Psa for the *Seasons* of *Life*

Ancient Wisdom for
Contemporary Living

A devotional by
Arnold R. Fleagle

honeycomb house
PUBLISHING

Psalms for the Seasons of Life

ISBN: 0-9753934-0-5

Printed in the United States of America

Published by

honeycomb house
PUBLISHING
3671 White Oak Drive
Norton, Ohio 44203

Editorial Consultation by David E. Fessenden

Editorial Assistance by Matthew A. Fleagle

04   05   06   07   08   5   4   3   2   1

Contents

Foreword

I love music, especially *gospel* music, which the Lord has allowed me the privilege of singing for the last 54 years. God has truly blessed as over and over through the years I have witnessed hearts renewed and lives changed through the gospel in song.

Because of my love for singing I have always been drawn to the book of Psalms. There is just something deeply moving about literally singing your heart out to the Lord as the psalmists did. Whether it was songs of joy and praise, or songs of hopelessness and despair, one tune runs through each and every Psalm. God is there, ever loving and ever faithful.

So when Arnie Fleagle wrote this devotional book on the Psalms, I was extremely proud that he allowed me the honor of writing the foreword. I have the distinct honor of knowing Arnie as my pastor and dear friend. I have tremendous respect and admiration for him. Not only is he one of the most anointed and dynamic preachers I have ever heard, he is also a wonderfully gifted writer. *Psalms for the Seasons of Life* is certainly strong evidence of this reality.

The insights the Lord laid upon Arnie's heart as he prayed through the Psalms are both beautiful and challenging. I firmly believe this is why I find myself going back to this devotional daily for strength and guidance. I know this book will minister to you as it has to me, and I pray that whatever "season of life" you may be in that you will always be able to "Sing, Sing, Sing!"

In His Service,

George Younce
Gospel soloist and member of The Cathedrals Quartet

Introduction

*T*he word *Psalms* in Hebrew means praises; in Greek
it means songs. Combine the two ideas and you will
find that "praise songs" aptly describes the basic
themes of the poetry and prose that Israel set to music and
used as a hymn book. The many writers of the Psalms (with
David the most prominent and prolific) were often harassed
and hounded, confused and critical, but they eventually
seemed to return to the summit of praise. So it should be in
our pilgrimage: though we taste of sorrow, we should finish
our course with the sweet morsels of joy on our lips!

The classic men of the Bible ran to the Psalms for their
inspiration in their greatest triumphs and tragedies. Jonah
quoted them in the fish's belly, Jesus in the Garden of
Gethsemane. Peter incorporated the Psalms in his marvelous Pentecostal sermon, and Paul included their wisdom in
his Roman masterpiece. Maybe we should find our way
there, too. These are ancient texts, but they are profitable
for contemporary living.

I have now been praying through the Psalms for over three years. The insights that the Lord has shown me are precious to me and I believe could be significant for you, as well. John Calvin wrote that the Psalms consist of "the anatomy of all parts of the soul" and I believe their truth addresses virtually every facet of the human experience.

I invite you to join me in this journey through *Psalms for the Seasons Of Life*.

Arnold R. Fleagle

DAY 1 ~ PSALM 1

The Choice of a Counselor

*Blessed is the man who does not walk in the counsel
of the wicked or stand in the way of sinners or sit in
the seat of mockers. But his delight is in the law of the
LORD, and on his law he meditates day and night.
(Psalm 1:1-2)*

The opening psalm of the Hebrew hymnbook is a theological divide: the first three verses are devoted to the saint, the next three to the sinner. It forms one of the Bible's most promising texts for believers, and one of the most harrowing for the unbeliever. There is no neutral ground, no demilitarized zone. You are either for God or against Him; an evergreen fruit tree or a piece of worthless chaff; bound for the promised land, or headed for unthinkable punishment!

This psalm begins with the word *blessed*, which in the original language is in plural form, for emphasis—how many times blessed is the man who avoids ungodly influences! But this positive beginning is followed swiftly on its heels by a warning about the power of negative associates and counselors. The axiom that in five years people will be products of the *books* they read and the *friends* they associate with is robustly endorsed by this psalm. Life is like a photograph—it is just as important what and who you leave out of the picture as what and who you allow in it.

"Bad company corrupts good character" (1 Corinthians 15:33). One bad apple really does make the whole bunch

1

bad. The first verse of Psalm 1 demonstrates that the progression of contact with the ungodly comprises a series of red flags—first a man walks with the ungodly, then he stands and finally he sits down. What begins casually leads to conversation and ends in confinement. Our circle of friends, sooner or later, becomes our circle of counselors. Whether this is a good thing or a bad thing depends on the kind of friends we have. "As iron sharpens iron, so one man sharpens another" (Proverbs 27:17), but dull iron makes for dull iron.

> *One of the barometers of spiritual health is a man's love affair with God's Word.*

One of the barometers of spiritual health is a man's love affair with God's Word. Psalm 1:2 paints a blessed man as one who delights in God's Word in daylight and through the night season. The blessed person assigns a place in his schedule for engagement with God's Word. Does your day start with a briefing from the Master's manual? Are you taking time to feed on His Word daily? The daily bread of the true believer is found in digesting the Word of God—and digestion takes time! The Bible must not be a quick-fix snack food, but a meal well chewed, enjoyed and savored.

This Bible is not a road map, but it is a compass and every committed believer must be riveted to and piloted by it—not detoured by a culture that is heading down a dead-end street. His flawless law leads to a formidable faith. His Word is the premiere counselor, "a lamp to my feet and a light for my path" (Psalm 119:105).

Thought

The answer to the question, "Who is my counselor?" also answers the question, "What is my destiny?"

Prayer

Dear Lord,

I realize that my companions have a large role in whether my life bears fruit or is barren. Please give me discernment as I choose my herds and huddles so that my journey will be favored by Your presence and Your sweet blessing. Enable me to influence others in such a way that I will be a help, not a hindrance, to their holiness and righteousness.

Day 2 ~ Psalms 3 and 4

A Strategy for Sleep

*I lie down and sleep; I wake again, because the
LORD sustains me. (Psalm 3:5)*

*I will lie down and sleep in peace, for you alone, O
LORD, make me dwell in safety. (Psalm 4:8)*

David was the most powerful personality of his era. As king of Israel, he embarrassed his people's enemies, extended the country's boundaries, and escalated the nation's wealth. However, he reveals in Psalms 3 and 4 that he was threatened by many adversaries. It is noteworthy that in both of these psalms his faith in the Lord and the protection the Lord provides him is demonstrated by *sleep*!

Sleep and rest are biblical trademarks of God's blessing. Psalm 127:2 declares, "He grants sleep to those he loves." However, this blessing is not always easy to grasp. The many stresses of our modern age have interfered with the rest of many a believer. Carloads of Christians toss and turn at night as they wrestle with realities that appear in a plurality of forms—sometimes human, sometimes natural, sometimes genetic, sometimes even demonic. The follower of Jesus Christ walks a narrow road lined with obstacles and opposition.

The superscription to Psalm 3 discloses that this writing occurred when David was fleeing from Absalom, his own son. Now that's a prescription for wrinkled bed covers! I cannot imagine one of my sons planning to force me out of my job so that he could be named my successor, yet this was the case with David.

Absalom coveted his father's throne. He questioned his father's justice, charmed the people with politician's kisses and lured away Ahithophel, his father's counselor. Absalom deceitfully asked his father's permission to go to Hebron, all the time with the secret purpose of forming an army to overthrow David. Absalom, whose name means "father of peace," had become his father's most dangerous predator. Can you imagine how David felt when the messenger brought the shocking news that "The hearts of the men of Israel are with Absalom" (2 Samuel 15:13)?

David's throne was threatened by the treacherous scheming of his own son, Absalom. How did David gain the strength to lead his people and be able to sleep at night?

How did David leverage this incredibly disturbing development to gain the strength to lead his people and be able to sleep at night? The two psalms contain his threefold strategy:

First, he passionately prayed (3:4; 4:1; 4:3). David communicated loudly and often because he fully expected the Lord to respond to his petitions. Do we pray with expectancy or just with panic?

Second, he had a high view of his Protector: "You are a shield around me" (3:3). The original Hebrew means a shield that completely insulated the warrior-king. Is the Lord inclusive in His protection of His people, or is He unable to secure our position? David understood what we must believe and live by—that nothing can reach us unless it passes through His holy hands.

Third, David committed himself to abandon fear (3:6) and tenaciously trust in the Lord (4:5). He had put his confidence in the One who specializes in deliverance (4:8).

The Great Physician wrote this three-part prescription for David to prevent him from experiencing insomnia: (1) passionate prayer, (2) correct theology, and (3) tenacious trust.

Jesus Christ made a beautiful offer to those who were worn out by the battle of life: "Come to me, all you who are weary and burdened, and I will give you rest" (Matthew 11:28). Come and experience sleep in the middle of troubled times. The anxiety and panic and torment over the difficulties of life yield little resolution or change. The Father and Son are waiting for someone to call to Them, someone to understand Who they are, someone to surrender the trouble to Them because he or she trusts in Their power to conquer whatever or whoever it is that surrounds him or her.

Augustine, the early Church Father, once wrote, "Our hearts are restless until they rest in Thee." May we comprehend that unchanging reality. The many adversaries of David were overcome by his one ally—his loving God!

Thought

The answer to the question, "Who is my source of safety?" also answers the question, "How well do I rest?"

Prayer

Dear Father in Heaven,

You are my protector and refuge. My life is challenged on many fronts, and at times, I look to myself and not to You. Forgive me for my independence and assist me in casting all my cares upon You and the Lord Jesus Christ. May I sleep well, knowing that You never sleep and that all things are small to You.

DAY 3 ~ PSALM 8

He Reigns, We Rule

When I consider your heavens, the work of your fingers, the moon and the stars, which you have set in place, what is man that you are mindful of him, the son of man that you care for him? (Psalm 8:3-4)

*I*n all literature no text more comprehensively paints the essence of the excellency of the creator God than Psalm 8. The psalmist spans the galaxy from the constellations to the crib of a tiny child to demonstrate the majesty of the Lord God Almighty. It is a sweeping, breathtaking song of grand and glorious admiration and awe. This psalm is designated an "envelope song" because it begins and ends with the same exclamation: "O Lord, our Lord, how majestic is your name in all the earth!"

Additionally, there is no more apt and concise synopsis on the creature we call man than in verses 4 through 8. In contrast to this incomparable God, man would seem to assume an insignificant place in the universe. But this psalm contends that man is but a hummingbird's eyelash below an angel, and his position on the planet is akin to God's position in the universe, one of dominion, power and authority. Hold on to your suspenders! This psalm is an elevator to our feelings, not only about the God we adore, but also the race to which we belong on earth.

This psalm is a gold mine of exalting God and elevating man. Like a master of ceremonies it presents the King and the sons of men that He has promoted from paupers to princes. This psalm assists us in answering Augustine's prayer: "O God, may I know myself, may I know thee."[1]

9

The glory of God in this psalm crosses the universe with light speed. The tail end of verse one finds God's glory above the heavens. It is higher than we will ever reach on this earth. It is farther than we will ever travel, until we are taken in death, or translated into eternity, like Enoch or Elijah. His name is majestic in all the earth, but earth is not sufficient to contain it. Our planet is like a small glass trying to hold oceanic waters.

Then the glory of God streaks back to the nursery. The excellence of God is found in the incoherent "ga-ga goo-goos" of the diaper set. It is not the cuteness of the little tykes that is being showcased here, but the fact that God can employ little creatures to still great enemies of His kingdom. The power and awesomeness of God is demonstrated in the weak things of this world. First Corinthians 1:27 notes this: "But God chose the foolish things of the world to shame the wise; God chose the weak things of the world to shame the strong."

A master craftsman can achieve greatness even though he uses the simplest tools to get the job done. When David faced Goliath, both the Philistine and Israeli armies must have labeled it the greatest mismatch of the ages. A gladiator from Gath named Goliath is challenged by a ruddy shepherd boy with a slingshot. Think back over David's words in First Samuel 17:45: "You come against me with sword and spear and javelin, but I come against you in the name of the Lord Almighty."

Do you see the strategy of God? The higher the odds, the more dramatic the demonstration of His majesty! When God wanted to pry Israel loose from four centuries of bondage in Egypt, He began with a baby hidden in the river. Moses, whose name means "out of water," was rescued by none other than Pharaoh's daughter. When God wanted to reveal His Messiah and proclaim Him to the world, He picked a young lady in Nazareth of poor peasant stock. She conceived and, after a long journey, delivered her baby in a small town called Bethlehem. What did you say was that baby's name? His name is Jesus!

As we face our giants and our empires, we should believe that even though we are outnumbered and the odds are stacked against us, God enjoys confounding the "Jimmy the Greeks" of this world. His glory is revealed in the cribs and cradles of the earth!

This psalm has been nicknamed "the astronomer's psalm." Most likely, David wrote it as he gazed upon the night sky and watched the stars wink at him. He is considering the heavens in verses 1 and 3. He is trying to imagine the incomprehensible God that has called him for service. He is surveying the incredible universe that God has designed and displayed for all mankind to behold. The cribs of verse 2 are replaced with the constellations of verse 3.

David was no different than the poets who have mused and dreamed about the night sky through the centuries. Many of us studied James Weldon Johnson's poem, "The Creation," which reflects man's preoccupation with the unlimited universe which envelops him. The universe is a miraculous tribute to our God—and we know the architect of the galaxies! We know the designer of millions of worlds. We live in a galaxy powdered with planets and stars, each one a brilliant shining tribute to our God!

At times we do feel like an atom in the immense cosmos, a single leaf falling to the ground in history's forest, unnoticed and ignored, a grain of sand on the endless shores of eternity. But we must *remember* that God *created us for a purpose*, and condescended to us in Jesus Christ.

Indeed, we are the visited race; this is the visited planet. And whatever inferiority complex has draped us, we must never forget God's love affair with us. He has made us, according to Psalm 8:5, just a hummingbird's eyelash below an angel, in His image, with dominion and power over the plant and animal kingdoms. He has put "all things under our feet." One writer put it this way: "Every dish of fish or fowl that comes to our table is an instance of the dominion man has over the works of God's hands."[2]

Yes, we are men, in male and female versions. Contrasted with God we are infinitesimal, but He is the potter, and potters take useless clay and manufacture masterpieces out of it. The Creator has spruced us up, and we creatures can change our world! So what if we think we are weak instruments? A toothpick driven by a tornado can dig its way into a tree. Don't underestimate what God can do with you or me!

Thought

The answer to the question "Can God use the ordinary to do the extraordinary?" also answers the question, "Can I be used in His divine plan, even though I'm just a man?"

Prayer

Dear Lord Almighty,

The oceans seem so vast, and my ship seems so small. Yet, according to Your Word, I am just a little lower than the heavenly beings. Guide me through the waters of this world and grant to me that I may reach the shores of Your Will for my life.

Notes

1. Augustine of Hippo, *Soliloquia*, book 2, chapter 1.
2. Charles Spurgeon, *A Treasury of David*, vol. 1 (McLean, VA: Macdonald Publishing, n.d.), p. 95.

DAY 4 ~ PSALM 14

A Foolish Heart

The fool says in his heart, "There is no God." They are corrupt, their deeds are vile; there is no one who does good." Psalm 14:1

A t Emory University in Atlanta, Georgia in 1963, Paul van Buren declared "that the word 'God' is dead."[1] The prestigious southern learning institution became the grave plot where God had been laid to rest. The denial of God's existence is an atrocious, ludicrous, and offensive assertion for devoted followers of the Christian faith, but to a world that has eaten at the tables of Altizer, Freud, Hegel, Blake, and Harvey Cox, and has been bombarded by a pervasive media that is almost exclusively atheistic or agnostic, this denial has become standard fare.

For you and I history is linear: it has a beginning and end. For most of our culture it is evolutionary, left to happenstance and chance, the dynamics of a societal and physical lottery. A Dutch philosopher, Herman Dooyeweerd, described history in these terms:

> *History has no windows looking out into eternity.*
> *Man is completely enclosed in it and cannot elevate*
> *himself to a supra-historical level of contemplation.*
> *History is the be-all and end-all of man's existence*
> *and of his faculty of experience.*[2]

We live in a world that is pregnant with the "there is no God" philosophy. There are no absolutes; morality is a personal and situational issue. Although the church is outnumbered, although there are plenty of "fools" saying "there is no God," I want to remind us of Thoreau's comforting assessment: "A man more right than his neighbors constitutes a majority of one."[3] We serve a faithful God in the midst of a planet populated by foolish hearts.

The fool is the man who denies that God exists. He lives his life independent of any creator, any revelation, any set of moral and ethical guidelines. He operates without restriction.

---

*The fool lives for the moment,
not for eternity.*

Probably the first thing we think of when we hear the word foolishness is a diminished intellect. Psalm 111:10 provides the primary test of intellectual capacity: "The fear of the LORD is the beginning of wisdom; all who follow his precepts have good understanding. To him belongs eternal praise." Those who do not believe in God are, as my mother-in-law so colorfully puts it, "dumb as a clam." To deny God's existence is irrational, but it is a prevailing mindset in today's world. How else could we explain such blatant and "stick your tongue out" responses to Christian teaching and lifestyles? The fool lives for the moment, not for eternity.

Someone has described an atheist as a person "having no invisible means of support." Those who operate independently of God, who ignore Him or fail to acknowledge His existence or control, develop the moral fragrance of a garbage dump. Their lives are repulsive, their ethics animal-like. Love turns to lust, loyalty to adultery, and generosity to greed. The milk has soured.

Without the road map, without the manual we call God's Word, without the Holy Spirit as pilot, modern man is bewildered and traveling at high gear in no clear direction. He has lost his way and has not consulted the compass. The fog is heavy, the highways are unmarked, and the hazards are many. Isaiah 53:6 reminds us that everyone is at one time a lost traveler: "We all, like sheep, have gone astray, each one of us has turned to his own way; and the LORD has laid on him the iniquity of us all." But, fools refuse to be found, and so they are at the mercy of a wicked world and do not have the assistance of a Heavenly Father to watch over them. They need to come home!

These foolish hearts have an appetite to devour the people of God. We are in spiritual warfare. There is a conspiracy of evil to confound the Christian agenda, confuse the Christian message, and confine Christian people. We are a target that makes the pagans of our culture salivate! Jesus clearly defined the antagonism that awaits us: "I have given them your word and the world has hated them, for they are not of the world any more than I am of the world" (John 17:14).

These foolish hearts are overwhelmed with dread (v. 5). The Hebrew for this description is "they feared a fear." Fools come to places of insecurity and uncertainty. Without a theology or a personal relationship with Jesus Christ, they fight their fears alone. They break into cold sweats! The boastful man has become the bawling child. The tough guy has become a squirming mouse. Somewhere, sometime, the fool needs more than human resources—but his access is cut off, the supply beyond his reach. He needs God, but he has severed himself from Him. What a pathetic end!

I remember my mother referring to the three R's: reading, 'riting and 'rithmetic. There are three R's adorning the end of this psalm, which lift up our heads and fill our hearts with renewed joy: refuge (v. 6), restoration (v. 7) and rejoicing (v. 7). They portray the benefits of a vital relationship with our God. We have a hiding place in Him, a hospital where the Chief of Staff can heal us of any deformity or infirmity, and a river of joy that is always flowing with promise!

The foolish hold in their hands a bunch of puzzle parts that will never fit together. We hold in our hearts the Holy Spirit of God, who created the puzzle in the first place.

Our world view is a theocratic one. Our God is in control. Our Jesus has come and demonstrated His authority over the physical, natural and demonic forces which operate within our sphere of existence. We cry out, "Thus saith the Lord!" We shout, "Jesus is the Lord of history!" We minister in the power of God who enables us to stand tall in a collapsing world.

Thought

The answer to the question, "Do I believe in God?" also answers the question, "What is the I.Q. of my heart?"

Prayer

Dear Lord and My God,

I submit to You that my desire is to have a wise heart. I want You to be the center of my Life. Reveal Yourself to me again and again, through the world around me, the Word before me and the Holy Spirit within me. May my lips and life demonstrate my determined commitment to follow Jesus Christ Your Son, and my Shepherd.

Notes

1. Eerdmans' *Handbook To The History of Christianity* (Grand Rapids: Eerdmans, 1977), p. 608.
2. Herman Dooyeweerd, as quoted by Herbert Schlossberg in *Idols for Destruction* (Nashville: Thomas Nelson, 1983), pp. 14-15.
3. Henry David Thoreau, *Civil Disobedience*, 1849.

DAY 5 ~ PSALM 19

Knowing God through Sky and Scripture

The heavens declare the glory of God; the skies proclaim the work of his hands. (Psalm 19:1)

The law of the LORD is perfect, reviving the soul. The statutes of the LORD are trustworthy, making wise the simple. (Psalm 19:7)

The Christian faith is born in the womb of revelation. Had God chosen to hide Himself, man would never have found Him. God chose, however, to reveal Himself, and this psalm of David focuses on two of the primary ways that we can see and know our Heavenly Father.

This capsule on God's revealing nature is built on two components, the skies and the Scriptures. What God has created and what God has written serve to disclose the divine Person and plan. This revelatory hymn moves us to the telescope as we look at the canopy of the constellations and then bids us reach for the microscope as we view the words of Holy Scripture and pan for their glorious gold.

The stars are God's oldest witnesses. They are a silent, shining tribute to His handiwork. Verse one is a classic case of Hebrew parallelism, where the same idea is stated in similar ways. The "heavens" and the "skies" are basically the same entity. This redundancy reinforces the psalmist's point: "Look at the sky and you will increase your perception of God Almighty!" During the French Revolution, Jean Bon St. Andre said to a believing peasant, "I will have all your steeples pulled down, that you may no longer have any object by which you may be reminded of your old supersti-tions." "But," replied the peasant, "you cannot help leaving us the stars."

Natural revelation is present both day and night (v. 2). This perpetual festival never ends. These time/light desig-nations of creation envelop us with God's presence. We may deny God, but we cannot *escape* God!

In my Father's world there is a single star we call the sun (vv. 4-6), which is an ambassador to all the earth. It is a solar cell of energy that races across the sky like a bride-groom coming out of his chamber. Every atom on earth is touched by its heat! It is a comprehensive messenger that is a bond slave to the God of the ages!

Creation reveals God's presence, but a more precise revelation is the Scriptures, which define in particular who God is, and what course man should take to reach Him and live in His image.

But there is a more precise revelation, which is *specific* in revealing this Creator—it is the Scriptures, which define in particular who God is, and what course man should take to reach Him and live in His image.

The latter half of the psalm is a writer's dream for one who loves to alliterate! Verses 7-14 extol the Scriptures as revealing God and His intentions for individuals who long to live in spiritual wholeness and holiness.

This Lord is a Lawgiver (v. 7). The Scriptures serve to convert the sinner to a saint. The verb here has the force of bringing back, like a shepherd's crook pulls in a wayward ewe. The testimony of God makes wise the simple! The dunce becomes the Delphi Oracle!

The scriptural statutes are right (v. 8). This leads to a rejoicing heart because our very lives are not grounded on the quicksand of speculation, but on the *terra firma* of God's infallible Word. Light dawns in the midst of heavy darkness and we exclaim, "Once I was blind, but now I see!" This is happy medicine from heaven which cheers the convert.

The Scriptures change us—our goals, our aspirations, our values. Where once we craved gold, we now crave God. Where once we craved food, we crave faith. These Scriptures are more to be desired than gold, and taste sweeter than honeycomb (vv. 9-10).

The Scriptures reveal God's convicting nature: they put pressure on us to change. They corner us! They flash before us like a yellow warning light to signal danger. The servant is warned, and his obedience leads to great reward (v. 11). In reference to the Bible someone has written, "Sin will keep me from this Book, or this Book will keep me from sin."

The Scriptures declare God's cleansing and forgiving nature (v. 12). At times our minds do misfire and we commit foolish, stupid, unjustified sins. The Word is like the laver, a polished metal bowl that held water at the tabernacle; the worshipper could first see his blemish in its mirror-like surface, and then be cleansed by its waters. The Word reveals and then removes!

The Scriptures correct and realign (v. 13). They make the downright upright, and the guilty innocent. They enhance our fellowship with man and our relationship with God. David's final prayer should be the goal for all of us—that the words of our mouths and meditations of our hearts be acceptable (v. 14). In *general revelation* and in *special revelation* may we be inspired from above and instructed from within to stand in His holy presence unashamed.

19

Thought

The answer to the question, "Do I daily see God in the skies and in the Scriptures?" also answers the question, "Do I daily increase my knowledge of God?"

Prayer

Dear Heavenly Father,

I stand in Your art gallery every day of my life. I am amazed at Your creation and it speaks of Your power and majesty. I also travel through Your Word each day and I praise You for its teaching and truth. Please continue to show Yourself to me through natural theology and through the treasures in Your written Word.

Journey from Lament to Thanksgiving

*My God, my God, why have you forsaken me? Why
are you so far from saving me, so far from the words
of my groaning? (Psalm 22:1)*

No Psalm is quoted more frequently in the New Testament than Psalm 22. It has been labeled "the psalm of the cross." Its original context addresses the disorientation and darkness of David's life. Its prophetic context wraps itself around the agony of Jesus Christ who became sin for us and died on the cross. Many of the realities of this Old Testament psalm become painful facts for Jesus as he endures the cross for the sake of God's fallen creatures. David cries out in his powerful lament, "My God, My God, why have you forsaken me?"

Jesus selected David's cry and made it His own as He was suspended between heaven and earth, as the blood congealed on His sacred skin, as the sweat rolled down His precious brow, as the people mocked and ridiculed His pathetic plight. God's Son would speak these words of loneliness and abandonment: "My God, My God, why have you forsaken me?" These are personal words, passionate words, piercing words, and they beg for an answer.

The answer is found in God's will. Sometimes His servants, His sons and daughters, and even His beloved, only begotten Son, experience hurt so that healing may come. God permits despair, disdain, and sometimes death to visit those He cherishes, in order to bring light and love and life.

David incorporates many expressions that describe the attack upon his body. As generations read the psalmist's descriptions, their minds have raced to the dear Savior who before His disciples "took bread, gave thanks and broke it, and gave it to them, saying, 'This is my body given for you; do this in remembrance of me'" (Luke 22:19). Long before Jesus came to earth, about one thousand years before our Lord's visit to our planet, David felt the brokenness of his own body. In verses 14 and 15 he presents a litany of excruciating torment. He depicts himself as "poured out water"; his bones are twisted out of joint; his heart has melted like wax; his strength is dried up like a broken piece of earthenware, baked in a Mediterranean sun; his tongue sticks to the roof of his mouth as if it has been clamped there, and he claims to be lying in the dust of death. This great warrior has become a man tortured to the point of being a spectacle.

The imagery David selects to portray his attackers is stunning. His adversaries are raging bulls, roaring lions, wild dogs—and they have pierced his hands and feet. The reader of this psalm almost wants to ask him to stop talking about such devastating circumstances, like a mother at the supper table tells her children to cease talking about gory details which threaten to bring indigestion.

We must move the video forward to Jesus, as the Gospel writers did, when they became journalists describing the agony of Jesus Christ. The scribes and Pharisees were bullish in their attempts to discredit His miraculous ministry and halt His holy crusade. Many wicked people plotted against Him. His hands and feet were pierced; his tongue was glued to His beautiful mouth and He confessed His dryness with the exclamation, "I am thirsty" (John 19:28). The garments which covered His body were stripped away and gamblers cast lots for the Savior's humble wardrobe.

Both David and Jesus tasted the bitterness of suffering; their bodies screamed with lacerating pain, and the Heavenly Father withheld His hand that greater good would be attained. The great king of Israel and the King of kings both groaned as their bodies were broken by the evil conspiracies of wicked men and because of the permissive will of God. For David, his brokenness would be answered with God's saving right hand; for Jesus, His brokenness would lead to the salvation of mankind.

David employed a very pitiful word picture to describe himself in Psalm 22:6: "I am a worm and not a man, scorned by men and despised by the people." The Hebrew word for "worm" is also used to describe the crimson crocus from which scarlet stain was extracted to color the robes of kings. This may well be a reference to the shedding of Jesus' blood. I can remember as a child watching worms as they innocently traveled on my sidewalks, and I relished catching up to them and squashing them until their blood burst out. Jesus became a worm who was sacrificed so that you and I would not have to be punished for our sins.

Certainly, the piercing of the hands and feet that David explicitly mentions in verse 16 describes the blood he shed in the hour of his despair. Jesus would also spill His blood on His journey to Calvary and He shed it freely on the cross. Isaiah would prophesy of the Messiah's piercing with these words: "But he [Jesus] was pierced for our transgressions" (53:5). The blood of Jesus was poured out, not because He had any sin, stain, or impediment, but to satisfy the requirement that was needed for the forgiveness of our failures.

Our spiritual ancestor David did not enjoy his suffering. And, as we listen in on Jesus' conversation with His Heavenly Father, we clearly comprehend the distastefulness of the suffering that He was to endure, and that He asked to escape from: "My Father, if it is possible, may this cup be taken from me. Yet not as I will, but as you will" (Matthew 26:39). Jesus desired to bypass the cup of suffering—so much so that He asked the Father two more times to forego

23

it (Matthew 26:42, 44). Yet, He submitted Himself to the Father's perfect, yet painful, plan.

Psalm 22 ends well. David proceeds to declare God's deliverance and reign over circumstances and nations. It is noteworthy that his final words are "He has done it" (22:31), which in Hebrew is one word, *asah*, which means "finished." In similar fashion, when Jesus is on the threshold of death on the cross, He uses one Greek word, *tetelestai*, which means "finished" (John 19:30).

This prophetic psalm speaks to us—indeed, shouts to us —that God has decisively dealt with our trauma and our transgressions. Our lament, like David's, has been transformed into a song of thanksgiving. A broken body and the shedding of blood, has ended at salvation! The broken have been blessed; the forsaken have been fortified; the hurting have been healed! Isn't that just like God? He turns thorns into thrones and crosses into crowns.

Thought

The answer to the question, "Why did David and Jesus suffer?" also answers the question, "Why do the righteous suffer?"

Prayer

Dear Father, the Lord Jesus, and the Holy Spirit,

Though my suffering does not approach the intensity of David or The Lord Jesus, I still have my moments of grief and disappointment that cast a shadow over my day. Make me strong in the darker days of my journey and lift my thoughts to the reality that the sun is always beyond the thunder clouds of my life.

A Sheep's Favorite Sermon

The Lord is my shepherd, I shall not be in want.
Psalm 23:1

Ｔhe survival of sheep is absolutely dependent upon shepherds. Sheep are unintelligent, prone to wander, lack defenses, are afraid of water, and are among the most helpless of farm animals. Sheep that have a good shepherd are guaranteed a happy existence, because it is the shepherd who sets the quality of life for those he tends.

Scripture portrays God's children as sheep, in both the Old and the New Testaments. Perhaps no other piece of literature in the world so beautifully portrays this analogy as Psalm 23. This is the cornerstone of David's writings. The message is calm and confident. It transcends the vicissitudes of life and ends with the sheep being brought home.

This psalm has been used to lead people into the inner chambers of the Kingdom. It has been employed as therapy for the fearful. It is whispered in the nursery to pacify the mother who wonders how her vulnerable baby will ever endure the chilly winds of this world. It is shared in the intensive care unit when the patient senses that man has done the maximum and there are no more options and no more alternatives. It is most frequently found in the funeral service because it treats death not as a house that we will dwell in, but a porch we will step off of into a new and better world.

If a survey could be taken, an animal's Gallup Poll of favorite sermons, I believe that the sheep would rate Psalm 23 as their favorite, with verse 1 serving as the title. There is no panic in this song from the heart of David, only promise and peace and a composure that men dream about. This is no illusion! If you have accepted God's love and forgiveness, you have a Shepherd who charts your tomorrows and provides in miraculous and eternal ways.

As man has increasingly defined himself by existentialism and humanism, he has moved away from God. David embraced God and made certain that those who read his writings understood that he was singular in his choice. He deployed a singular article as he opened the psalm, which narrows the field to one Lord. His term of choice for God is the word *Yahweh*, the name God chose when He introduced Himself to Moses. A broad definition of this title would be, "*I-am-becoming-everything-you-need* is my shepherd."

What an incredible description for a shepherd! This keeper of the sheep has inexhaustible resources and can satisfy abundantly every demand a sheep could ever have. If we could really believe in God's absolute ability to fill the bill whatever the crisis or circumstance, what a bright world this would be! Watch people as they try to "do it themselves," or turn to some other limited human to resolve their dilemma, or hope for "Lady Luck" to be the winning difference in their lives. Is it any wonder that this world's inhabitants seem in so much turmoil? David, with the softness of Indian silk, states, "The Lord is my Shepherd."

The analogy of shepherd came out of David's own livelihood. David's biography in Scripture portrays him, in his early years, as an admirable shepherd. He even stood as savior for his sheep against the likes of a lion and a bear—that is beyond the call of duty! But with all of David's admirable skill and understanding of shepherding, we can appreciate this analogy even more than the writer, for we are witnesses of the *Chief Shepherd*, Jesus Christ.

The New Testament portrays three situations where Jesus functioned as a shepherd toward his sheep. These scriptural scenarios reveal the shepherd as acting in three ways:

First, the shepherd sees his sheep; second, the shepherd seeks his sheep; third, the shepherd sacrifices himself for his sheep in order to save them. As Jesus is studied the meaning of the psalm swells like a sponge tossed in a bucket of water. "The Lord is my shepherd" becomes pregnant with powerful new meaning!

In Matthew 9 Jesus is blitzing the countryside, preaching and teaching, healing every disease and infirmity, and His fame is spreading like a forest fire. In the midst of this campaign he looks around Him and His eyes focus on the people and their desperate plight. Matthew 9:36 states, "When he saw the crowds, he had compassion on them, because they were harassed and helpless, like sheep without a shepherd." This shepherd keeps a watchful eye on His sheep, and even when they are scattered across the valleys and mountains of this world, His eye is still observing them, and not only registering their plight, but being moved by their pain and confusion.

In Luke 15, Jesus has mingled with the tax collectors and sinners, the social outcasts and deviants of that day. The Pharisees slam Him for His company, and then follows the parable of the "ninety and nine." A shepherd with a flock of a hundred sheep discovers that one is missing. In our contemporary era, majority rule and bottom-line thinking would have dictated that the shepherd ignore this one sheep and concentrate on the remaining flock. I must confess that this does make sense to me. As the parable unravels, however, the shepherd sets out to find this stray and leaves behind the entire flock, to save *one solitary sheep.* He retrieves this lost lamb, assumes the lamb's burden by placing it on his shoulders (probably because the sheep couldn't even walk home), and then calls his friends and neighbors to rejoice with him over the reclamation of this single sheep. We have a shepherd that seeks.

In John 10, Jesus gives commentary on His role as shepherd. It is an astonishing profile of His love which stretches even into the dark corridors of death. Four times in this passage, Jesus speaks of death as essential to the Good Shepherd's role. He distinguishes the shepherd from the hireling, who stays by the sheep until the wolf comes, and then takes his money and races away. Jesus tells us that the sheep He cares for find life! Most shepherds raise sheep for one reason: to make a profit. Eventually they slaughter their sheep. This Shepherd, out of His love, changes places with His sheep—the sheep live and He forfeits *His* life!

The little word "my" in verse 1 makes this psalm up-close and personal. There is no swallowing of our identity in a crowd of sheep. This one-to-one relationship has such an amazing therapeutic value to our sanity and security when we realize we are Jesus Christ's personal trust, His pet project.

If Jesus is not who He said He is, then we sheep might as well start our pathetic bleating and begin our slow and steady procession to the slaughterhouse. But if He is the Good Shepherd and can deliver what He promised, then we are in good hands and our manifest destiny is this: "Surely goodness and love will follow me all the days of my life, and I will dwell in the house of the Lord forever." The sheep smiles today, because he knows the Shepherd is already preparing for tomorrow!

Thought

The answer to the question, "Who is my shepherd?" also answers the question, "Will I have everything I need?"

Prayer

Dear Shepherd,

My gratitude cannot be expressed in any language for the ministry that You invest in my life. I am so lost and bewildered without You. Keep me close to You that I may experience the incredible benefits of following You.

Day 8 ~ Psalm 23

A Sheep's Diary

He makes me lie down in green pastures,
He leads me beside quiet waters,
He restores my soul.
He guides me in the paths of righteousness
for his name's sake. (Psalm 23:2-3)

Psalm 23 opens with a *grand affirmation*: "The LORD is my shepherd, I shall not be in want." The rest of the psalm details why the sheep is so ecstatic about the Shepherd, and forms the diary of a sheep, with personal observations about the One who watches over him.

This diary is best understood in light of the many liabilities of sheep, such as: they resist lying down; they fear running water; they have difficulty getting back on their feet if they roll over; they walk habitually in the same paths, destroying forage and forming ruts in the soil.

In the late morning environment of the East, sheep face a scorching sun. They need to lie down and be still. Sheep, however, obstinately refuse to take this therapeutic action, stalled by four compelling fears. First, they fear that lying down makes them vulnerable to wolves and other predators. Second, they fear being attacked by the other sheep. Third, they fear that petty flies and parasites may annoy them. Fourth and finally, they fear going hungry; an empty stomach keeps them on their feet grazing.

If they do not rest in the midst of these fears, they will eventually be destroyed by exhaustion and fatigue. The good shepherd allays their fears and satisfies their needs so that the sheep assume this vital rest position. In our frantic age, we sheep also resist rest and refreshment in God's love and providence, but we need parentheses and pauses in our lives. Vance Havner said, "Jesus told us to come apart and rest, or else we will fall apart!" Today's sheep must believe in the Shepherd's ability to deal with the hostile world around them, in His ability to watch while they recline.

That He lays His sheep down in green pastures is crucial to our concept of the Good Shepherd. Green pastures induce heavy milk flow, help sheep fill up quickly and lie down sooner, and prevent the animals from becoming scrawny and sickly from long searches for rare patches of turf on a desolate terrain. Sheep tend to choose inferior pastures. The shepherd, however, works hard to discover the prime pastures that will supply his sheep most abundantly.

Years ago I was mother and father to our oldest son, Matthew, while his mother was away. I was responsible to prepare the place where he would lie down for a nap. My little "sheep" was quite distressed when he walked in and found that the "shepherd" had not made the bed, and his stuffed animals were not in proper position. I didn't want to be bothered with mattress covers, sheets, and blankets. I didn't want to puff pillows and position special partners. But I now understand that in order for my sheep to sleep, he wants everything orderly, wrinkle-free, and properly placed. God understands His sheep. And I am told that shepherds must sometimes develop their pasture, which means clearing, plowing, tearing out, seeding, irrigating, and husbanding the grass. My Shepherd has gone to great lengths to assure that where I lie down is redemptive and restful to me.

Sheep fear running water; they are poor swimmers and their wool is dead weight when wet. The shepherd must find a still pool where the flock can quench their thirst.

The Good Shepherd knows our weaknesses and how to compensate for them. He provides for our essential needs, and not at the expense of our own well being. In our spiritual journey there are tempestuous times that prevent us from being nourished and strengthened. The Shepherd leads us into the quiet valleys and bids us come to the tranquil pools of the prayer closet, the devotional study of the Bible, the soothing Christian book, the sharing of thoughts with a Christian friend, the glimpse of a quiet sunset, the musing of time and eternity under a starlit sky. God provides those special pools of promise and peace, without which we sheep would soon dry up and exhaust our spiritual supply!

Augustine said, "My soul is restless until it rests in thee." Tolstoy spoke of man's thirst for God. And Pascal said, "There is a hole in every man's soul and only God can fill it!" Rest is found, thirst is satisfied, the vacuum is filled by God's presence and power—His Holy Spirit. We need to turn away from a world in turmoil, from the tyranny of the urgent, to those streams that slowly filter in the deserts of this world, to those pools of Holy presence.

The old English term "cast down" describes sheep that have turned over on their backs, with feet projected heavenward. They are often unable to turn themselves upright. When we do a spiritual "belly-up," we have a Shepherd who can restore us to our feet. Our sheeply tendencies lead us to roll over sometimes, but the Lord Jesus, being the Good Shepherd that He is, bends down to our difficulty and applies His strength to get us vertical again. Jesus combs the fields of this world watching for "cast down" sheep. He is able to deliver us from our belly-up times if we let Him.

In the East, shepherds go ahead of their flocks, because sheep have an overwhelming Achilles heel—they get lost! Isaiah 53:6 accentuates this weakness: "We all, like sheep, have gone astray, each of us has turned to his own way."

In contrast, Jesus declares, "I am the way, and the truth, and the life" (John 14:6). This is our steadfast hope, that our Shepherd is not leading us to a dead end, but in right paths, so that eventually we may get home again!

We sheep need to leave the leading to the Lord. Leadership depends on the ability to see ahead, to chart a course which in the long run is superior to all others. The short-sightedness of sheep (they can see only 10 or 15 yards), puts them in peril. Our Shepherd can see farther than we can. *We must not judge God's paths until they are complete.* What may appear to be the wrong direction, may in the long run be the way home. F.B. Meyer put it this way:

> *Not always beside the gentle stream, but sometimes by the foaming torrent. Not always over the delicate grass, but sometimes up the stony mountain track. Not always in the sunshine, but sometimes through the valley of the shadow of death. But whichever way it is, it is the right way, and it leads home.[1]*

Do you need rest? He makes me lie down!
Do you need freedom from your fears? He leads me beside the still waters!
Do you need to be made whole? He restores my soul!
Do you need to be led to glorify Him? He leads me in the paths of life!

Thought

The answer to the question, "Who am I following?" also answers the question, "Will my diary be a delight or a disaster?"

Prayer

Dear Shepherd,
There are many times I give up on green pastures and still waters. Help me look beyond the five senses to the faith reality that exists in and beyond this world. You know exactly where to lead Your sheep, so don't let me relish my independence. I don't want to walk in circles; lead me in Your path of righteousness that ends in a glorious Heaven!

Notes

1. F.B. Meyer, *The Shepherd Psalm* (Chicago: Moody, 1976), pp. 48-49.

DAY 9 ~ PSALM 23

A Sheep's Destiny

Even though I walk
through the valley of the shadow of death,
I will fear no evil, for you are with me;
your rod and your staff, they comfort me.
You prepare a table before me
in the presence of my enemies.
You anoint my head with oil; my cup overflows.
Surely goodness and love will follow me
all the days of my life,
and I will dwell in the house of the LORD
forever. (Psalm 23:4-6)

*A*s we look over David's shoulder, we notice a change in his diary. There is a shift in his references to the Shepherd from the third person, *He*, to the second person, *You*. An intimacy, a closeness seems to draw the Shepherd and the sheep to each other in the final entries. Our sheep is describing enemies—including the final enemy, death—yet his constant confidence in the ability of the Shepherd to bring him home is not diminished. Sheep do wander, but this particular sheep knew his final destiny: "I will dwell in the house of the LORD forever!"

There is now a new urgency, a critical test for the sheep and his Keeper. The valley of the shadow of death poses a monumental test as the sheep makes his journey to the sheepfold. It is a part of every sheep's path, and it is essential that the Shepherd overcome this perilous place!

Several observations leap out from the diary. The landscape darkens in this valley of death. The sheep no longer runs or frolics; he slows to a walk. The terrain is not clearly seen and the dangers not clearly known. It is the Shepherd's

33

vision that must compensate for the impoverished vision of the sheep. Why can you have confidence in your Shepherd when you travel through such a frightening place?

First, Psalm 139:12 teaches this truth about the Lord: "darkness is as light to you." The brightness or the dimness of our paths does not affect our Shepherd's vision in the least. He is not handicapped by the amount of light!

Second, He has traveled this path before and knows each step to take. Our Good Shepherd pioneered a path through this valley when He was crucified and entered death's domain. As the old hymn says, "My Lord knows the way through the wilderness; all I have to do is follow." He has taken the sting out of this dark and foreboding valley.

Third, the Shepherd knows that this is the way home. Death is the gateway to life! While on a family road trip, we had to pass through tunnels on the Pennsylvania Turnpike. Our children saw us move into darkness and wondered what had happened. We assured them that this was a part of going home, and soon they saw light!

The word "shadow" is crucial to an understanding of this psalm. A shadow is not the real thing. A dog's shadow cannot bite; a tree's shadow cannot fall and hurt you. And death's shadow cannot destroy you, because Christ met and defeated death. We only encounter the shadow! According to the sheep, the valley of death has lost its terror.

One more point needs to be made concerning shadows: there must be light for a shadow to exist. No darkness is too deep to keep the Good Shepherd from lighting the way.

The sheep sees two instruments—the rod and the staff —as consoling friends. The first was a heavy, hard club, two feet in length, which served as a weapon to ward off predators. Another use of the rod was to count the sheep.

The eight-foot staff was employed to discipline sheep, but also to hook them back from danger. The shepherd's crook has snatched millions of sheep from steep cliffs and deep waters. The crook becomes a life buoy!

The staff was also used for digging. The shepherd "prepared a table" for his sheep by going ahead of the flock and rooting out poisonous shrubs and thorny plants that grew in the sheep's tableland. The staff was a vital weapon in the shepherd's arsenal as he engineered the sheep's survival.

David could look back at the first communion service, held in Egypt the night the death angel swept over the land and touched the firstborn of every Egyptian household. On that night in an enemy land, the Israelites sat at a table and a lamb was eaten, a sacrificial animal which provided food and redemption from the Pharaoh's henchmen. Today we look over our shoulder at the Lord's Supper, which found Jesus eating a religious meal "in the presence of His enemies." This is a memorial feast that commemorates Jesus' conquest of our enemies, even that most stubborn enemy, death. Jesus has weeded out the opposition and prepared a table of mercy and grace, at which we may feast at any given moment. We may be surrounded by our foes, but their cause is lost, and the war is won!

When the sheep pass the shepherd at night he is sensitive to their need for anointing. There are many parasites that infest a sheep's head. Sheep are so tortured by these parasites that they rub their heads against hard objects such as trees, rocks, and posts, often going into hysteria trying to get relief. At the first sign of the infestation the shepherd applies oil to the head, which serves to soothe the wounds and prevent further flies from infecting the sheep.

Sheep get very thirsty in the arid climates of Holy Land. Human sheep get very thirsty in the hostile climate of this world. David often watered his sheep with an overflowing jug of water. The sheep's thirst was appeased, its need satisfied. Jesus said, "those who hunger and thirst for righteousness . . . will be filled" (Matthew 5:6). We don't need to fear dehydration if we are close to our Shepherd.

This diary ends on the most encouraging note: we make it home. In a world like ours, where everything is unstable

—where the only thing you can depend on is that nothing can be depended on—in this kind of fluctuating world, we long for permanence. We grasp for eternity, and in this psalm we hear eternity's whisper. The sheep's ears are eager to hear the Shepherd's song, "It won't be long until My steps will lead you home."

The shepherd leads the sheep, and goodness and mercy follow him. F.B. Meyer called goodness and mercy the "celestial escorts." Charles Spurgeon called them "God's footmen," alluding to the two men who took their place behind the coach in his day. They jumped out to open the door when the coach stopped. They ran ahead into inns to prepare the room. They made the journey smooth!

We sheep scare easily, but the Shepherd is always there and will lead us home! This beautiful psalm has given peace to the pilgrim for over twenty-five centuries! It still means as much, maybe more, than it meant to David on the Middle Eastern plain that supported his sheep. It lives for you today.

Thought

The answer to the question, "Will the Good Shepherd walk with me through the valley of the shadow of death?" also answers the question, "Will I be full of fear when I walk through it?"

Prayer

Dear Lord Jesus,

You are the Shepherd I need to navigate me through life. Increase my faith in You so that when my time comes to walk through the valley of the shadow, I will be strong and courageous, knowing that You have led me all the way and that You can lead me through that day of darkness into glorious light!

DAY 10 ~ PSALM 25

A Student Seeks the
Ultimate Scholar

Show me your ways, O LORD, teach me your paths;
guide me in your truth and teach me, for you are God
my Savior, and my hope is in you all day long.
(Psalm 25:4-5)

David is in jeopardy. His circumstances are life-threatening. In this psalm he briefs the reader with a description of his dilemma. He is a candidate to be shamed (vv. 2, 20); he needs forgiveness from his iniquity (v. 11); he feels like he's already caught in a snare (v. 15); he is lonely (16); and the number of his enemies is multiplying (v. 19). Abraham Lincoln's comment, "I have often been driven to God by the overwhelming sense that I had nowhere else to go," seems to fit David like a custom-made suit. Like a marathon runner in a blinding snowstorm, he is incapable of finding his way!

Why does our hero approach God? In this medium-sized passage of Scripture, David provides the rationale. The Lord has a reputation for great mercy (v. 6). A lost or wayward sheep is much better served by a compassionate shepherd than a cruel one. The expectation of the one praying is that God will remember him from the street corner of His love (v. 7), rather than from the scrapbook of David's sins (v. 7). Our faith must always look to the goodness of our Savior rather than to the guilt of our many sins. The individual who majors on his bleak past puts a lid on his unwritten future. David's hope (vv. 3, 5, 21) is riveted not only to mercy and love but to God's goodness (v. 7), His faithfulness (v. 10), His name (v. 11), and His marvelous grace (v. 16)—that is, His propensity to give us what we don't deserve. Our appeals must pass through the friendly confines of God's attributes, not the minefields of our past mistakes. Our spiritual ancestor had the discernment to approach God regarding His difficulties *on the basis of Divine character*, not human failure.

The most recurrent theme in this psalm of petitions resides in the author's passionate desire to be led by the quintessential teacher, by the ultimate scholar.

Though David requests deliverance from sin and his opponents, the most recurrent theme in this psalm of petitions resides in the author's passionate desire to be led by the quintessential teacher, by the ultimate scholar. We identify with David as his personal instincts and experience are insufficient to function as a dependable instrument panel. The relentless pursuit of God's way and will prompts David to engage in a semantic smorgasbord of terms to communicate to the Lord his desperate demands to be shown the way. "Show me" (v. 4), "guide me" (v. 5), "teach me" (v. 5), David says, and his assessment is that the Master teacher "instructs sinners" (v. 8), as well as "guides and teaches" the humble His way (v. 9).

Will the Lord respond favorably to the urgent cries of His child? Again, the answers are provided by David in his text. The humble (v. 9), the obedient (v. 10), and those who fear the Lord (v. 14) can be confident that the questions of the searching head will be met by the answers of a heavenly heart! Why not approach the Lord and allow Him to use His impeccable instrument panel to pilot your life onto His runways?

Thought

The answer to the question, "Who is my teacher?" also answers the question, "Is the course worth it?"

Prayer

Dear Lord,

I am ready to learn from the Master Teacher. Without You I will fumble and fail, but with You I believe I can pass life's course with flying colors. Please show me, guide me, and teach me. I seek to honor You and be an honor student for You.

DAY 11 ~ PSALM 30

Exalt the Lord, Lift Him High

I will exalt you, O LORD, for you lifted me out of the depths and did not let my enemies gloat over me.
(Psalm 30:1)

A ll men worship! They worship something or some-one. It is both true and tragic that the majority of men have bowed down to other gods. The words of Hosea 8:4 have a painful and familiar ring: "With their silver and gold they make idols for themselves to their own destruction." Where is our allegiance? Who or what do we spend our time, talents and treasures upon?

Traditionally, when we hear the word "stewardship," we think of our pocketbooks and wallets. But proper teaching on stewardship appeals to a total life lived for God, to His ultimate and majestic glory. God's people march to a different drummer. Our standards are higher and our aims holier. We are not satisfied with the dusty lowlands of this world. You and I should be climbing higher and in the process becoming a "living sacrifice," a goal which Paul characterized as "reasonable service," or the expected response.

There is a danger in this type of emphasis. Some will say the call is too strong, the questions too personal, the cost too high. Yet God's expectation is a high road, a lofty ideal, an incredible adventure to be lived.

The author of Psalm 30 is David. The reason for its composition is debated, but the most convincing arguments suggest it was composed for the dedication of the temple. This beautiful passage later was incorporated into Jewish liturgy to commemorate the exile experience of Israel. Just prior to the time of Christ it was employed at the feast of Hanukkah, which marks the rededication of the temple (165 B.C.) after its desecration by Antiochus Epiphanes just three years earlier. (This enemy of Judaism confiscated the holy vessels, captured the temple treasury, built a pagan altar on top of the holy altar, and sacrificed swine upon it.) This psalm has tremendous historical overtones attached to it.

The application for us is essential. Exalt God! Even when there is peril—praise Him! Even when there are enemies—exalt Him! Even when you get content and self-confident, and because of that smugness end up in some kind of sticky dilemma—repent and serve Him as Lord! David is shouting through the centuries that God is the first Person of our lives and that we should be investing our lives for His glory, not our own. Why? For He alone turns wailing into dancing, and dark nights into joyful morning!

David knew the joy of victory and the agony of defeat. The rationale for his exaltation of his God is in the initial verse of this psalm. "You lifted me out of the depths" is a watchword woven throughout Old Testament poetry. The word "lifted" in its original meaning denotes the pulling up and down of buckets in a well. This God of Abraham, Isaac and Jacob had elevated him from distress to delight.

David had flirted with death and felt its icy breath, yet his extremity was met by God's opportunity and he was delivered. David pledged himself to exalt God. It was a decision of volition: "I will exalt You, O LORD." He made it a life principle to place God in the *numero uno* position—to give Him preeminence. His praise was built upon a foundation of deliverance. Those who reflect upon the manifold mercies of God will be thankful people who cheerfully and willingly give their time, talents and treasures to Him.

David honors God in 30:5 for the contrast between His holy anger, which is momentary, and His divine favor, which stretches over a lifetime. You and I weep; David wept; but the weeping nights are countered by the rejoicing which comes in the morning.

For me, January and February are the night seasons of any year. Winter shortens the daylight; snow brings hazards to travel; nature has lost its wardrobe; and people see less of each other than at any other time. What keeps me going is the realization that all things pass, for God has made spring to follow winter. Robins gather; trees start budding; and the air takes on a moist and fresh feel. This hope of spring is such a life buoy to the doldrums of the winter season.

It is interesting that the Hebrew word for "joy" can be used for the ringing cry of sorrow *or* joy! So, we could say that to the extent that we lament our sorrows, God will compensate in full with laughter for our successes.

Thomas Brooks wrote a beautiful thought in Spurgeon's commentary on the Psalms:

> *Their mourning shall last till morning. God will turn their winter's night into a summer's day, their sighing into singing, their grief into gladness, their mourning into music, their bitter into sweet, their wilderness into paradise.*[1]

However, deliverance has within it the seeds of destruction. David confesses his smugness, even arrogance, as he remarks, "I will never be shaken (v. 6)." The "comfort zone" is dangerous territory. Just because you stand doesn't mean you can't fall, warns Paul in the New Testament. John Phillips observed, "As soon as things go our way we tend to become careless of spiritual things." Spurgeon cautioned, "Few of us can bear unmingled prosperity."

Our favor, firmness and faith are directly proportional to our relationship with and dependence upon God. When we talk of self-reliance rather than reliance upon Him, we are "an accident waiting to happen." When we turn our back on God, it won't be long until we are *flat* on our back!

David found himself in a number of jams. We are not

sure which "jam" he is referring to in Psalm 30, but it must have been a humdinger. We are fairly certain he contributed to its severity. With Hebrew parallelism in great supply, he inquires of God, "Is it better for me to die? And if I do, who will praise You—will the dust?" David resorts to a plea of desperation—he cries, "Help!"

David's zeal for God can be traced to the Almighty's ability to turn the worst to the best, to step into our lives and make a welcome, wonderful exchange! There is a rainbow after the rain. The wailing is turned into dancing. The sackcloth, or mourning clothes, have been removed, and joy is draped over David's heart. This is a message we need to remember: it ain't over till God says it's over!

David's heart would not be silent. He exalted God—and though he never lived to see the temple that this psalm was probably used to dedicate, his penchant for praise outlived that legacy of stone and wood.

Thought

The answer to the question, "How soon will I exalt the Lord and trust in His mercy?" also answers the question, "How long will I stay in the depths of despair?"

Prayer

Dear Lord,

You are my helper and healer. Remind me that my independence will only lead to sorrow and my dependence upon You will always lead to joy! I pledge to exalt You and to sing of Your love forever.

Notes

1. Charles Spurgeon, *A Treasury of David*, vol. 1 (McLean, VA: Macdonald Publishing, n.d.), p. 51.

Sinners Can Be Singing

Blessed is he whose transgressions are forgiven,
whose sins are covered. Blessed is the man whose sin
the LORD does not count against him and in whose
spirit is no deceit. (Psalm 32:1-2)

*T*his psalm begins as it ends—in joyful, jubilant song. Not since Psalm 1 has David begun one of his hymns with "Blessed." There is so much triumph as Psalm 32 opens its front door to us. It is not the song of a self-righteous Pharisee, but of a pitiful publican. It is not the music of an elder brother who has pleaded his merits, but the melody of a maligned prodigal son who has proclaimed his despair and found deliverance. The publican has been justified; the prodigal is eating prime rib in a regal robe, with his flashing ring gleaming in the sunlight!

Three striking words (vv. 1-2) pave the way for rejoicing in the heart of David. The first word, *forgiven*, is a song in the night season. It means to take away, to carry out of sight. That which is despicable and disgusting is no longer present. The filthy rags are carted away by God's laundryman, and a new robe of righteousness is wrapped around the naked man. Forgiven is one of the sweetest-sounding words in our vocabulary and in this psalm the *uptight* man becomes *upright* when he experiences it!

The second word is *covered*. Sin can be covered. Sin is like a scarlet stain, deeply imbedded in the fabric of our souls. Men and women have cosmetically dealt with the stain of sin, but it wears its way through our camouflage. The grace of God has been distributed through the blood of a sacrificial lamb. The symbol of life has been recognized by God as a suitable covering for the sin-blemished soul. David had experienced the scarlet stains being made whiter than new-fallen snow!

The third word is *count*. Our sins are no longer listed on our record! The person is guilty but the record is destroyed. There is no penalty because there is no record. The festival of praise is triggered in verses 1 and 2 because the guilty is innocent; the pauper is now a prince; the sentenced sinner has now been knighted a saint!

Sin can shame a singer to silence (v. 3). The songs of silence are devastating in the hymnbook of our lives when there is transgression in our hearts. Confession is imperative—or pathetic living is imminent. David's portrait of the silent sinner is incredibly intense. His bones waxed old. There is a physical manifestation that results when people feel guilty; they lose their vitality, energy and enthusiasm. Unconfessed sin can often produce psychosomatic by-products. David says that God's hand of conviction is heavy upon him night and day. There is no break, no vacation, no intermission. The reminders of our sin seem to keep turning up like bad pennies. This is a loving function of our heavenly Father so that we will not continue with the cancer, but get the surgery. Our minds do not need to be tormented and harassed by sin, but if we are silent, time provides no refuge. David uses the analogy of the almost intolerable summer in Israel, when temperatures soar upward, the wells go downward and dust chokes a man's palate. David seems to be choked by his silence; there is drought in his soul.

Verses three and four draw a pathetic picture of a soul unwilling to confess. There is no refreshment for the body, no rest for the mind, no relief for the soul. When believers clam up and praise diminishes to a trickle, there is just cause for lips to spring forth in confession, and then springtime will come. Dead churches are full of silent confessors!

Augustine said, "The beginning of knowledge is to know thyself a sinner." On a sunny day in Chicago in September 1972, a stern-faced, plainly dressed man stood on a street corner in the busy Chicago loop. As pedestrians hurried by on their way to lunch or business, he solemnly lifted his right arm, pointed to the person nearest him, and intoned loudly the single word "GUILTY!" Then, without any change of expression, he resumed his stiff stance for a few moments before repeating the gesture: the inexorable raising of his arm, the pointing, and the solemn pronouncement: "GUILTY!" The effect of this strange *j'accuse* pantomime on passers-by was extraordinary, almost eerie. They would stare at him, hesitate, look away, look at each other, and then at him again; then hurriedly continue on their way. One man, turning to the one who told me this story, exclaimed, "But how did he know?" No doubt many others had similar thoughts. How did he know, indeed?

David's awful agony over his sin was conquered only when he acknowledged it. Verse 5 is a beautiful expression of a man freed from bondage: "I acknowledged my sin to you and did not cover up my iniquity. I said, 'I will confess my transgressions to the LORD'—and you forgave the guilt of my sin." David sent a telegram to God to report his transgression. So many of us have stopped sending telegrams to God; we are too reluctant to take care of our sins.

Confession is an arrow in the Christian's arsenal. David was not ashamed to admit that he stumbled along the way, and that he depended on God to make things right. When the storm clouds are in the skies of your life, get into the ark of safety! And you will shout as David in verse 6, "When the mighty waters rise, they will not reach [me]." You will say as David did in verse 7, "You are my hiding place." God does not shoot His wounded—He heals them!

The only time God speaks directly in Psalm 32 is in verses 8 and 9. It is as if He takes the microphone away from David and speaks to the audiences of the ages. His message is simply: *you sinners can be students!* He passionately tells us that He wants to direct our steps and lead

47

us in wonderful ways. But, we are often like horses and mules which need bits and bridles to get them going in the right direction. God understands us and He knows it is best to have our guilt removed and our sins taken away.

This psalm has a happy ending. There is gladness and rejoicing! But remember, David acknowledged his sin prior to the party. We really need to bring confession out of the Christian catacombs, dust it off, and use it frequently in our faith. If you are on an empty tank, and a gas station is right beside you, what should you do? If you are on an empty stomach, and a full refrigerator is in the next room, what should you do? If you are troubled and tentative in your faith because of some past act, some questionable thought, some unkind word, what should you do? You will not enjoy a season of thanksgiving until you have shared in the cleansing that follows confession. *David was a great sinner, but also a great confessor.* Are you singing and celebrating the riches of your God before a sad and sorry world? Let us lay aside every weight in our lives and the sins which keep us silent!

Thought

The answer to the question, "Why are you not praising God?" also answers the question, "When is the last time you confessed your sin?"

Prayer

Dear Heavenly Father,

I choose to be a singer in my life and not a silent sinner. Please do the laundry in my life so that my heart may be pure and my song might be heard. Remove any sin, stain, or impediment, and make my song a composition of praise and celebration to You!

DAY 13 ~ PSALM 34

Praise That Never Quits

I will extol the LORD at all times; his praise will
always be on my lips. (Psalm 34:1)

David sets before us one of the incredible goals for his life in Psalm 34:1—perpetual praise, or *praise that never quits*. This goal was the by-product of two monumental experiences in the young man's life in the land of Gath. The superscription tells us that this Psalm of David was written when he changed his behavior before Abimelech, King of Gath, and pretended he was insane.

Imagine David's heart melting as he remembered his confrontation with Goliath of Gath. In this same land he entered Israel's "Hall of Fame." It was here that, as the youngest of eight sons, he brought a snack to his brothers who were fighting the powerful Philistines. It was here that there came to his ears the sarcastic dares of a mammoth warrior who challenged any Hebrew to match strength against him in a struggle to the death.

It was on the soil of Gath where Goliath plummeted to the earth following David's bull's-eye to the giant's temple. It was here where Goliath's blood dripped to the dust after David retrieved the mighty soldier's sword and whacked off his head. Gath had been the land of conquest. It was easy to sing praise songs in that circumstance.

But David's victory led to perilous times. The best of times degenerated into the worst of times. Conquest became calamity! Saul, fearing the young upstart was a threat to his throne, began a series of attacks upon the shepherd boy's life. Two times Saul thrust his javelin at David. In a more subtle move, the king set him out in the battle's forefront, hoping to make him a heroic casualty. Eventually, David found himself a fugitive, harassed and hounded by Saul's army and on the king's "most wanted list." These assaults drove David to the land of Gath where he was discovered and his life hung in the balance before King Abimelech, whose nation still remembered the slaying of their legendary warrior, Goliath.

David finds himself in severe straits. Realizing the desperation of the moment, the *giant killer* stoops to pretending he is a *lunatic*. The shepherd boy who did not fear Goliath feared Abimelech. The one who shook his fist at a giant is now making marks on the gates of the doors with his fingernails. The young man who verbally spat at Goliath's arrogance, now allows his spittle to drip down his beard and intensify his portrayal of a crazy man. Abimelech bought the performance and chased David out of Gath.

> *In the midst of David's failure, a resolution was shaped in his soul: "I will extol the LORD at all times, his praise will always be on my lips."*

The sad scenario must have swept over David like a bitter November rain. His soul was soaked with the embarrassment of his cowardly choices. In the midst of his failure, a resolution was shaped in his soul. "I will extol the LORD at all times, his praise will always be on my lips." David engraved upon his heart what we must engrave upon ours. The weather may change, from sunshine to showers, but the weather in our hearts can be continually fair. If we really trust God, if He is really in control, then He is sovereign in both the day and night seasons.

David's commitment in Psalm 34:1 rings with authority. "I will extol the LORD" is a steel statement of his posture toward life's peaks and pits. The will is involved in such a high plane of Christian living. This is an unconditional, unqualified posture of praise.

This quality of perpetual praise that David is talking about is found frequently in the Word. In Jonah 2:9 we read, "But I, with a song of thanksgiving, will sacrifice to you. What I have vowed I will make good. Salvation comes from the LORD." Submerged in a fish's belly, Jonah resolved to praise the Lord. Daniel responded to Darius' document, which would send him into the lion's den, by praising the Lord. "Now when Daniel learned that the decree had been published, he went home to his upstairs room where the windows opened toward Jerusalem. Three times a day he got down on his knees and prayed, giving thanks to his God, just as he had done before" (Daniel 6:10). Paul and Silas were singing at midnight in the Philippian jail and the keeper of the prison found Jesus that night!

This attitude of perpetual praise is not an option in Holy Scripture—it is a commandment. The New Testament plays this tune again and again. First Thessalonians 5:18 tells us to "Give thanks in all circumstances, for this is God's will for you in Christ Jesus." Listen to Paul in Philippians 4:6-7: "Do not be anxious about anything, but in everything, by prayer and petition, with thanksgiving, present your requests to God. And the peace of God, which transcends all understanding, will guard your hearts and your minds in Christ Jesus." *Praise leads to peace.*

Hannah Whitall Smith said, "The soul that gives thanks can find comfort in everything; the soul that complains can find comfort in nothing." One preacher said, "Praise is the lubrication that keeps your bearings from burning out!"

Thought

The answer to the question, "Do I praise God in stormy weather?" also answers the question, "Is my praise song perpetual or partial?"

Prayer

Dear Heavenly Father,

I desire that my praise will not have a short shelf life. Enable me, please, to manifest perpetual praise. Help me to have fair weather in my heart regardless of the circumstances that surround my life.

Time Is on God's Side —and Ours

*Do not fret because of evil men or be envious of those
who do wrong; for like the grass they will soon
wither, like green plants they will soon die away.
Trust in the LORD and do good; dwell in the land and
enjoy safe pasture. (Psalm 37:1-3)*

David contrasts the brief career of the wicked with the eternal inheritance of the righteous in this strategic psalm which helps the believer cope with the prosperity of those who do not serve God. Time is a crucial component of his argument, because time is on God's side. As we observe the "haves and have-nots" it does appear that the unbelieving definitely have an edge in the areas of leisure and possessions. We sometimes ask the Lord, "Why do those who dishonor You seem to do better in life than those who honor You?" The answer, according to Psalm 37, is, "It's just a matter of time!"

Three times David will present the injunction, "Do not fret." Two of the three instances cast the wicked in a very short-term position of success. The second verse of the psalm demands that the Christian take the "long view" of assessment. The wicked do prosper but they are like grass which springs up quickly and soon withers away. The ninth verse also frames the success of the wicked in a very short-term scenario. Evil men do succeed for a season, but they will be cut off, a concept which occurs four other times in this psalm (vv. 22, 28, 34, 38).

The law of recurrence demands that we take a serious look at this prediction and promise. Yes, wicked men prosper, but they do not inherit the land and possessions like the righteous. The law of recurrence operates in behalf of the righteous for they are predicted and promised this reality of <u>inheritance</u> six different times (vv. 9, 11, 18, 22, 29, 34).

David states that if we persist in fretting about the wicked, we become like them. He shows us the end of the journey when we fret, namely, we start to act evil.

The third time David challenges the believer not to fret is fascinating, because he catalogues not the situation of the wicked; instead, he states that if we persist in fretting about them, *we become like them.* In verse 8 he shows us the end of the journey when we fret, namely, we start to act evil. The wisdom of these "fret not" admonitions is so empowering when we realize that the wicked who flourish have such a short time to savor it.

In verses 3-6 David gives three counter-activities and their dividends during this temporary distortion which features unbelievers in an enviable position of success. Verse 3 directs the believer to *trust in the Lord and do good.* Despite this apparent unfairness—the prosperity of the ungodly—the saints are to be tenacious about their trust in the Lord. And the lifestyle of the saints is to feature good deeds —holy deeds which manifest His will in wicked times. This translates into dwelling in the land with safe pasture.

When many readers encounter verse 4 they focus on the last half of it: "and he will give you the desires of your heart." What is so often forgotten is the initial half of this equation: "Delight yourself in the Lord." As we engage and encounter the Lord our joy levels escalate and we experience the ecstasy of His presence which enables us to embrace His Word, His will, and His way. Out of this personal relationship with the Lord we come to want what He wants, and therefore His desires become our desires. And since His desires are fulfilled, we find the gratification of our desires because they were extrapolated from His mind and heart through our engagement with Him.

A third counter action to keep us strong and stable in times like these is to commit our way to the Lord. The word *commit* in the Hebrew means "to roll upon." We can figuratively picture in our minds the rolling onto the Lord our prayers, hopes and dreams, which seem in the short term to be sabotaged by the success of the wicked. We are invited by Peter in the New Testament to "Cast all your anxiety on him because he cares for you" (1 Peter 5:7). This is a liberating exercise of faith in God.

The psalm *begins* with an undesirable scenario; evil men are making a huge profit and having tremendous favor with their endeavors. But, the psalm *ends* with the righteous being delivered from the wicked and possessing God as their refuge and stronghold. The believing heart must recognize that the unfaithful and unbelieving are like grass which withers quickly and like smoke which vanishes away.

Over time those who "do not fret" and who trust, delight, and commit, find themselves holding the deeds to all good and precious things. Wait patiently and do good deeds, and soon the time will come when the people of God receive their incredible inheritance through Jesus Christ, God's Son!

Thought

The answer to the question, "Do I fret much?" also answers the question, "How much do I trust in the Lord?"

Prayer

Dear Father,

Give me the eyes of faith that look at this world, not just through the five senses, but through biblical lenses that convert any situation into a win for You and your children. Build into my inner man a steel-like confidence that tenaciously holds onto the principle that "all things work together for good!"

The Waiting Game

*I waited patiently for the LORD; he turned to me and
heard my cry. (Psalm 40:1)*

Psalm 40 deals forcefully with the issue of waiting on
God. If you are like me, you would rather *run* than
be on your *knees*. Waiting is anathema to my 4th-
gear, Type-A, hyperactive lifestyle. David was a winner for
God, but in this psalm he applauds the discipline of waiting
before winning. Scripture is sprinkled with tales of those
who ran ahead of God, who jumped the gun, and then were
shot by that same gun. "There is a time for everything, and
a season for every activity under heaven" (Ecclesiastes 3:1).
This truth is for all of us who have difficulty playing the
waiting game.

The English text of Psalm 40:1 does not transmit the
emphatic statement of David relative to waiting. The Hebrew construction is intense. A literal rendering would be,
"Waiting, I waited." If you go back in your memory to the
time you came home way late for your mother's fine din-
ner, you might hear her say again, "I waited and waited and
waited." This is the sense of this Hebrew phrasing. Daniel
Creswell described this type of waiting as *"vehement so-
licitude."* This is long-term, tie-a-knot-and-hold-on waiting. Have you been there? Are you standing there now?
David empathizes with you, for he knew the feelings and
frustrations of prolonged expectations.

Those who do not wait we may characterize as "green
apple eaters." They couldn't wait until the time was ripe
and the fruit was fully ready. They have tasted the bitter-

ness of "green apples." Adam and Eve couldn't wait until they tasted the tree of life. If they had refrained from the tree of knowledge of good and evil, they would have existed eternally without knowing the death angel's touch (see Genesis 3:22). Achan couldn't keep his hands off a Canaanite garment, some silver and gold, so he was exterminated. Saul rushed into battle and rushed out of his kingship because he couldn't wait for Samuel's blessing. Judas Iscariot, his messianic expectations shattered by Jesus' servant mentality, couldn't wait for God's conquest to take its rightful course, and so he betrayed his Master and committed suicide.

One of the classic verses of the Scriptures is Galatians 4:4: "But when the time had fully come, God sent his Son, born of a woman, born under law, to redeem those under law." *God has a timetable*, and we must trust Him to do things in the best chronological order for the best results. David waited fourteen years from his anointing to the time he assumed the throne. Joseph waited thirteen years from his sale into slavery until Pharaoh made him the number-two man in Egypt—that's a long wait from the pit to the pinnacle. Jesus Christ, a man pregnant with power, lived in obscurity until He reached thirty years of age and then he came forth from some insignificant Galilean town to shake the very foundations of the universe.

"Waiting" is part of God's training process; it is served at His training table. Waiting is a form of *spiritual dialysis*. We are renovated and revived through waiting.

It is illustrative that the Hebrew word for waiting in Psalm 40:1, *qawa*, means line. I couldn't help thinking of the fishing line. You can't throw your line in the pond and pull it out ten seconds later. David is saying, "I waited and waited for the big one, and finally I caught him!"

As we pursue our agenda during the waiting period we must be prepared for the chuckles of the opposition. In Psalm 40:15 we find David's foes saying, "Aha, aha."

David is steamed about it and prays that God may choke them on their laughter. This double "aha" appears three times in the Psalms, the other two being 35:21 and 70:3. Some scholars relate this to the prophetic passion of Christ.

We must respond in faith to the frivolity of our enemies. I remember when the insurance estimator came to assess the damage to our new church, which had collapsed under the harsh winds and snow of January 1978. As we walked up a wind-bitten hill to the debris, he made this remark: "Reverend, maybe you are praying to the wrong God!" I wanted to push that overweight critic to the ground, but I replied something to the effect that God was not finished with us yet. In time, God's work was restored, the people were vindicated, and the church had the last laugh!

We are waiting with the knowledge that God is working out His sovereign plan. You see, the dice of life are loaded. Romans 8:28 tells us that desired ends, designed by a divine and loving Father, are destined to become reality. We wait in confidence because we believe and know and stake our victory on a faithful God!

As we are waiting, this psalm reveals that God is working. He is inclining His ear, bringing us out of miry clay, putting new songs in our heart, and opening our ears to hear clearly His matchless Word.

Is it possible to live with such assurance? This has been personified in many faithful men and women. One such example is discovered in Eugene B. McDaniel, who was shot down over Vietnam. In his book, *Before Honor*, he describes his six-year imprisonment in a communist camp. Recognized for his heroism in the face of torture and extreme suffering he wrote,

> *As I grew older in the faith, I came to realize that optimism was solidly rooted in faith in God—the optimism that worked, that is, and any attempt to build up a positive attitude apart from faith could only carry one so many miles. Believing in God's positive attitude toward me, that He*

*wanted the highest good for me, was the only way I could
face each day with confidence.*

In McDaniel we hear the distant echoes of a man named
David. I waited and I waited and I waited, but I was sure
that God was working out His will for my life; I knew that
He was thinking about me.

We can say with David, "The Lord be magnified!" With
every other substance or living thing, magnification illumi-
nates flaws; with God it only *enhances* our awe for His perfection. "Wait for the Lord" (Psalm 27:14).

Thought

The answer to the question, "How long does it take me
to trust God when I encounter a fearful situation?" also answers the question, "How many moments of my life will be
spent unproductively?"

Prayer

Dear Father,

I am a clock watcher. Even though I know that You are
never early or late, I often attempt to hurry Your timetable
and hasten Your plan. Teach me that waiting is a spiritual
discipline and help me today to exercise that discipline in
my daily lifestyle.

DAY 16 ~ PSALM 48

Passing the Baton of Blessing

For this God is our God for ever and ever;
he will be our guide even to the end.
(Psalm 48:14)

A gene is a minute piece of a chromosome that heavily influences inheritance and development. Genes pass on traits, colors, and other factors of life forms. There are also spiritual genetics that are transferred from one person to another, passed from one generation to the next. The Jewish people were committed to the older generation mentoring the younger generation, and they made spiritual genetics a high priority in their culture.

In his book, *Educational Ideals of the Ancient World*, Williams Barclay cited the three goals for the Jewish father: "to instruct his son in the law, to bring him into wedlock, and to teach him a handy craft."[1] So the Jews told stories and passed on the theology of the one true God through oral tradition. (Remember, the printing press was not invented until the 1400s).

What are we passing on? Do our little children hear about answers to prayer that redirected our fortunes and reinforced our faith? Are the youth of our time acquainted with the divine moments that emerged because of our heavenly Father's intervention?

In Psalm 48, the sons of Korah, appointed by David to serve as the Levitical choir in the temple, give us a taste of spiritual genetics. In this psalm, they talk about God's royal city (1-3), God's redemptive portfolio (4-11), and God's resilient leadership (12-14). Comparing this to our time and our genetics we would say that we should talk about the *places* that God has manifested Himself in our lives, the *pictures* where God's redemptive portfolio has been very evident to us as He actively engages in our lives, and the *people* who have given us examples of grace-filled, merciful and godly living.

In Psalm 48:1-3, the Hebrews are called to remember God's royal city. It is described as His royal seat, a place of joy, beauty, and strength. There is spatial significance for the Hebrews in respect to God's royal city, and in our lives there are those strategic places of divine encounter where we meet with God, where we worship God, where we are convicted by God and then cleansed by God for service to Him. In our lives, we must, like the Jews, call the next generation to the special places of God's indwelling and intervention.

Psalm 48:4-11 features God's redemptive acts. Although the Jewish opponents were unified, the text reminds the reader that the Jewish opponents fled in terror. Like the Egyptians, the opponents of the Promised Land were scattered and destroyed. Therefore, by virtue of this record, the Jews hear with their ears and see with their eyes the works of God. In verse 9, they are called to meditate, to picture, to formulate God's scrapbook. In verse 10, it is reported that because of God's acts His praise extends to the far corners of the globe.

Also, there is reference in Psalm 48 to God's resilient leadership in verses 12-14. The Hebrew in verse 13 literally means "the generation behind." We are charged by the Lord to leave a legacy of faith and to tell the narratives of His divine work among us. Not to do so is to handicap the next generation, moving them farther away from Him and from His actions in their lives. A very interesting Hebrew formation is found in verse 14; in it we are told this God is forever and ever, and He will be our guide even to the end. *Three* different Hebrew words testify to His permanence. This is a great God, the one true God, most worthy of praise. This eternal and everlasting God exists in contrast to the plants around us and the skies above us and the oceans before us, which are all limited and finite and mortal.

Each generation must commit to making sure that the next generation understands the true and right concept of God. If those genetics are passed on correctly, the next generation will have a much greater opportunity to become a generation of righteous people who manifest integrity and holiness before their world. The genes are being passed and so the question must be asked, what kind of genes are they?

Thought

The answer to the question, "What type of spiritual genes are being passed on to the next generation?" also answers the question, "How much will God's people impact the next generation?"

Prayer

O Lord,

Help me to pass the baton of blessing to the children and grandchildren of the next generation, to make absolutely sure that they are connected to their Creator and Savior! I do have stories to tell to young minds and soft hearts. May these glimpses of God not remain hidden, but may they be released to inspire a new inventory of strong and courageous disciples!

Notes

1. Williams Barclay, *Educational Ideals of the Ancient World* (Grand Rapids, MI: Baker, 1959, 1974), p. 16.

DAY 17 ~ PSALM 51

The Journey from Darkness to Dancing

*Wash away all my iniquity
and cleanse me from my sin.
For I know my transgressions,
and my sin is always before me.
(Psalm 51:2-3)*

As David sings for us in Psalm 51, it is the autumn of his biological life. He is 50 and counting. His youth is behind him, his twilight years before him. In this psalm it is also autumn in David's soul. The tree which boasted luscious leaves and ornamental fruit is now barren, standing in the midst of brown foliage and rotten crops. David is now singing, "Lord, bring back the springtime."

David's untimely affair with Bathsheba had collected sinful baggage. He had lied, conspired and murdered. It had tarnished his testimony and still mars the majesty of his monarchy. Someone has said, "Sin is like a greased slide. Take one step, and the next thing you know you are at the bottom looking up." This is the psalm of a king on his knees in the mud-hole. Sin has heaped dark clouds of anguish on top of his life. His tears are many; his pillow at night has become like a stone; sunny days bring no consolation to his inner man.

The first twelve verses of Psalm 51 comprise a classic course in confession. David communicates insights which we can apply to our own times of confession, when we ask in faith for forgiveness because we know we have blown it, and blown it badly.

David is tormented and tortured by his sins. His approach to God opens with an immediate appeal to the mercies of God. God's mercies are in multitudes, and that thought counteracts in his mind the multitudes of sins he has accumulated. He forsakes his own merit; he lays aside his crown; he assumes the kneeling posture of the publican in Luke 18:13, who prayed, "God, have mercy on me, a sinner." Jesus told of this man's justification, and the future held the same destiny for David as he threw his dilemma on the grace of God.

Confession is the key to the front door of forgiveness and restoration.

It is crucial to note that David did come out and acknowledge his sin. In Psalm 51:3 he is explicit in his self-condemnation. Many brothers and sisters have stood on the front porch of forgiveness. They have seen their violations, they are aware of the consequences, but they cannot confess—and this act is the key to the front door of God's taking back the disobedient.

A strategic theological thesis surfaces in Psalm 51:4. David sees sin as an offense to God. A pure, holy, righteous God has been the object of his errant activity. When Joseph was tempted by Potiphar's lustful wife, Joseph refused her overtures by saying, "How then can I do this great wickedness, and sin against God?" (Genesis 39:9).

The prodigal son's reply to his father as he returned home was phrased like this: "Father, I have sinned against heaven and against you. I am no longer worthy to be called your son" (Luke 15:21).

As we view sin as an affront to the Most High God, who stands as pardoner and executioner, we sense its grim consequences to our lives if it remains unconfessed. We must take our eyes off of our existential, horizontal world, and look up to an eternal, ineffable, only wise God.

His solicitation for purging by hyssop is a direct flash-back to the cleansing of a leper. In Leviticus 14:10 the leper is sprinkled with water and blood by a hyssop instrument in order that he may be cleansed.

His reference to being "whiter than snow" is one of the most graphic expressions of forgiveness in the Bible. Snow is so white it is sometimes difficult to gaze upon, and the cleansing that David seeks is that of new-fallen snow. Isaiah 1:18 is the best known expression of this analogy:

> *"Come now, let us reason together,"*
> *says the LORD.*
> *"Though your sins are like scarlet,*
> *they shall be as white as snow;*
> *though they are red as crimson,*
> *they shall be like wool. . . ."*

Scarlet is the most difficult color or stain to remove from fabric, yet when the Lord is finished, its hue is a magnificent white. Hallelujah!

As this psalm unfolds, David seeks an anointing which leads to full acquittal from his pain and spiritual suffering. His ears want to hear the joyful sounds of life again. His bones want to be mended (v. 8). He wants the creative God to construct a clean heart, and to renew a healthy, steadfast spirit within his breast (v.10). He does not want to be expelled from God's presence, nor the Holy Spirit to be sent away from him (v. 11). He passionately longs for the joy bells of salvation to resound throughout the landscape of his life (v. 12). And history's hindsight confirms that the gracious God responded to David's agonizing confession and lifted him up from disgrace to a new relationship with his loving Lord. David's feet danced again the celebration of a man whose guilt was vaporized by the love of God!

Thought

The answer to the question, "Did I confess my sin?" also answers the question, "Is it winter or spring in my heart?"

Prayer

Dear merciful Father,

I approach Your purity with my impurity, Your holiness with my hollowness, Your perfection with my flagrant imperfection. Please let the snows of grace blanket and cover the darkness of my rebel heart. I long to dance again and praise Your acts of love that transform my despair to delight, and my brokenness to wholeness.

The Transgressor Teaches

Then I will teach transgressors your ways,
and sinners will turn back to you.
Save me from bloodguilt, O God,
the God who saves me,
and my tongue will sing of your righteousness.
(Psalm 51:13-14)

*I*n less than a year David has taken a nosedive from the joy of victory to the agony of spiritual defeat. His spiritual stock has plummeted further than a stock market crash. His afternoon gaze upon an incredibly beautiful woman named Bathsheba led him to leave a trail of sins which would shock even the contemporary mind. David fell from the penthouse to the poorhouse.

Psalm 51 distinctly divides into two sections. The first twelve verses major in his petitions to God to remove the sins which have contaminated his soul. Adultery, lying, drunkenness, murder—can this be the slayer of Goliath, the accomplished musician, the unifier of kingdoms? Yes, it can, and yet David looks to his God for an answer to his anguish. His heart of stone has now turned to water; his pride has been exchanged for humility; and his angry lips now acknowledge his many sins.

The final seven verses of Psalm 51 show the upside of David's unfortunate lapse into sin. He is anticipating a day of deliverance, a recital of praise, a type of worship which is true, authentic, and most of all, acceptable to God. There is a bright tomorrow for the sinner who will "cash in his sinful stock" and see his spiritual broker, Jesus Christ. Crashing can be followed by cleansing. It's snowing in heaven, even today, and our confessions unzip God's skies of mercy and grace. Let the snows come, and let them cover the soiled landscapes of our heart. David found out that *grace can erase disgrace!*

David is going to cash in on the school of experience. His fall will lead to others' faith.

As David turns the bend in this confessional psalm he anticipates a teaching ministry. "Then will I teach transgressors your ways; and sinners will turn back to you" (v. 13). David is going to cash in on the school of experience. His fall will lead to others' faith. Paul labeled himself "the chief of sinners," yet he became the greatest teacher of Christianity in the history of the church.

Think over the words of Jesus as he addresses an overconfident Peter who is about to eat his words of intense allegiance to his Master by denying Him repeatedly. Our Lord turned to Peter and said, "And when you have turned back, strengthen your brothers" (Luke 22:32). Peter's confession and repentance would put him in a place where he could encourage others who had fallen.

David would not waste this lesson on himself, and neither should we miss an opportunity to instruct others in the priceless lessons learned through the grid of our temporary failures. David is going to teach, and beyond that he is going to testify of God's righteousness. His sins had muzzled his mouth and trapped his tongue. God expects this kind of "out loud" dividend. He does not forgive us solely for our own benefit, but so that we may spread His awesome love abroad through the witness of our words! When was the last time you shared from the depth of your heart what God means to you or has done for you? God does not depend on a silent majority! We are to be a vocal majority.

David's anticipatory posture of complete forgiveness not only inspired him to teach and testify, but also to worship in truth. For many months he had worshipped like the Pharisees, who walked around like whitewashed tombs—pretty on the outside, but inside housing dead men's bones.

David shared in verses 16 and 17 the thesis that God does not delight in sacrifices offered by men who are not pure in heart. In other words, the *heart bleeding* is better than the *animal bleeding*.

When David speaks of a broken and contrite heart, he uses a Hebrew word for contrite which means "crushed." David brings a shattered heart to God which makes his sacrifices legitimate and legal. Spurgeon said: "A heart crushed is a fragrant heart." David knew this well and wrote it into the theology of this confessional: "A broken and a contrite heart, O God, you will not despise" (v. 17).

You can fool some of the people some of the time, but you can't fool God one single, solitary time! True religion springs from a right relationship with the Father in heaven. And that right relationship is only possible because God's grace can erase our disgrace. "His love has no limit, His grace has no measure," as the old song says.

I found a prayer by F.B. Meyer to which I believe David would shout "Amen!"

> *If my soul has turned perversely to the dark;*
> *If I have left some brother wounded by the way;*
> *If I have preferred my aims to Thine;*
> *If I have been impatient and would not wait;*
> *If I have marred the pattern drawn out for my life;*
> *If I have cost tears to those I loved;*
> *If my heart has murmured against Thy will,*
> *O Lord, forgive.*

David's story had a heinous beginning, a hurtful middle as he wrestled in anguish, but a holy ending. He knows his heart has been shattered like a mirror hit by a sledgehammer. He knows that God has promised to honor this type of confession. Don't chastise yourself for your sins; don't chain yourself with their memories; and don't spray yourself daily with their dingy odor. Come and appeal to His mercies; let the invisible mantle of "heavenly snow" cover your life, and you will teach, testify, and worship Him in Spirit and in truth!

Thought

The answer to the question, "What happens following God's forgiveness of my sin?" also answers the question, "How many sinners will I teach?

Prayer

Dear Restorer of the fallen,

I bow my heart low before You and I submit myself as one who stumbles too often and fumbles too many times in the game of life. In the next few moments, refurbish my tainted soul so that I might testify to others that You have recreated in me a new heart. May I regain the teaching credentials of an obedient disciple and lay aside the sad legacy of a wayward child.

DAY 19 ~ PSALM 56

Fear Is a
Four-Letter Word

When I am afraid, I will trust in you. (Psalm 56:3)

F ear is a four-letter word. It is a threat to our worship of God; in fact, if our fears grow large enough, they will dominate our lives and usurp our faith in the one true God. That is why God is so anti-fear.

If one verse were to be lifted out of this psalm as the primary text, it would be verse 3. It is often included in the little Scripture books for children that are sold in Christian bookstores, as well it should be. It was a part of our Bible memorization program in the early '60s at the church I attended, and I'm glad it was. It is a good verse for both children and adults to learn, because it addresses a crucial aspect of the Christian life.

This verse acknowledges that Christians do have experiences which breed fear into their breasts, but it also promotes a cure. "When I am afraid, I will trust in you." We are challenged to stop looking at the fearful things, and start casting our destiny on a faithful and loving God!

The background of this psalm is found in First Samuel 21. David proceeds to the city of Nob and meets with Ahimelech the priest. He is hungry and asks for bread. Unfortunately, the priest did not own a bakery, and the only source of this commodity was the worship bread, also known as the shewbread, which was kept inside the temple. The priest gives David the special bread, because it is being replaced with new hot bread.

David makes a second request of the religious figure. He is in need of a sword, to which Ahimelech replies, "The sword of Goliath the Philistine, whom you killed in the valley of Elah, is here" (v. 9). David receives this famous saber and resumes his flight from King Saul.

However, he runs from Saul right into the Philistine army and their king, Achish—a classic example of "jumping from the frying pan into the fire." Imagine David trying to disguise himself from the Philistines of Gath as he is now in possession of Goliath of Gath's sword! The servants recognize him. What will he do?

He does not challenge the king of the Philistines as he did the gladiator Goliath. He does not scream, "The battle is the Lord's!" He resorts to an Oscar-winning performance. He acts like a madman before this royal personage, making marks on the doors of the city gates with his fingernails and letting saliva run down his beard. Achish labels him insane, and is so disgusted that he lets him escape, because he does not want this bizarre personality in his home. It was not pretty, but it worked, and David begins again his trip to the throne of Israel.

Out of this Halloween-like experience, David pens a psalm detailing his dilemma, which resulted in a frightened hero being delivered in an unorthodox way. David was fearful. He admits to this fact in Psalm 56:3. The word he uses for fear is a fascinating one. It is first used in the Bible in Genesis 3:10 when Adam tells God that when he heard God's voice in the garden after tasting the forbidden fruit, he was afraid.

The word for fear, *yare*, is used not only in negative ways but also to express worship. It spans the emotion of fear, as well as the mental anticipation of trouble, reverence or awe, righteousness or piety, or formal religious worship. Interesting, isn't it, that fear and faith are related. What we fear can become for us a worship experience. Fear and faith are cousins.

David's fears were legitimate. The psalm reveals his slanderers are pursuing him all day long. They twist his words. They have devoted their lives to creating a successful conspiracy to derail him and destroy him. They are committed to ambushing him and severely altering his destiny. David's fears were rooted in a frightening reality, but it was not a reality that preempted the presence and person of the Most High God.

In the twenty-first century our fears are just as real and just as justified. We face such Philistine enemies as prolonged sickness, vocational distress, monetary shortages, unsaved family and friends, sometimes even the assaults of brothers and sisters in the family of God. We must confront these challengers and challenges. If we are going to witness effectively to a world that is lost, and if we are going to impact family, friends, and church, we must divert our energies spent fearing the secondary sources of our security, and invest our faith in a God who is in control.

David's solution is simple to discern. He appeals to the mercy of God in his opening words: "Be merciful to me!" Our Lord loves to demonstrate His mercy. By appealing to His endless, infinite storehouse of mercy, you open the door for God to display His beautiful character in an ugly situation.

David transfers his emotions from a fear tract to a faith tract in verse 3. This is the antidote, the answer: the greater our faith, the smaller our fear. And faith dissolves doubt, as the morning sun dissolves the morning fog.

David reaffirms his trust in God, and then makes a crucial affirmation. "I will not be afraid. What can mortal man do to me?" (v. 4). There are men who can wound us, even kill us. Yet, David displays almost an arrogance about this. He knows that God can preserve him if He so chooses.

We sometimes fear to the point of weeping and our prayers rise with salty tears to the heavens. David requests that his tears be put in a bottle. The word used in First Samuel 16:20 and Joshua 9:4 means "wine bottles." God knows all your pain; it is as precious to Him as fine wine. Have you ever cried enough to fill a bottle? Remember that a God who cannot forget recalls those tears.

David gets hold of himself in this psalm and realizes that God is on his side. Psalm 56:9 conveys the assurance of this passionate believer that his prayers will be answered.

The Bible tells us that we live in a physical world, but the ultimate realities are spiritual. We do fight battles, but if we dig deep enough we will discover that they are all spiritual in nature.

David completes his psalm with thanksgiving and praise. He is looking over his shoulder in Psalm 56:13, seeing another recital of God's saving power. He has emerged out of the darkness of despair to the light of the living.

If the Lord is in your life, you will still fear, but that fear will be dismissed as you gaze upon Him and replace your fears with faith in His character! If the Lord is not in your life, and you do not know Him personally, then you have a right to be afraid, and your fears should be terrifying, because you stand alone at the Day of Judgment.

Thought

The answer to the question, "When I am afraid, who do I trust?" also answers the question, "How quickly is fear chased from my mind and heart?"

Prayer

Dear Lord,

There are times when my fear swells slowly and other times when it spikes dramatically. I know these times will come to me and I cannot sidestep their reality. Give me the courage to step from fear to faith! May the darkness give way to the dawn because of my trust in You!

The Senior Psalm

Do not cast me away when I am old;
Do not forsake me when my strength is gone.
(Psalm 71:9)

My wife has spent most of her nursing career in geriatric care, that is, the care of the elderly. Advances in medicine have extended the human life span, but that translates into coping with old age and all its downside for an increased number of years.

Living into our eighties or nineties does not guarantee a great quality of life or even new bricks added to our noble legacy. I remember that Vance Havner once prayed, "Lord, don't let me live long enough to do something stupid and that's what I'll be remembered for." I think many people can attest not only to the humor of that prayer but its validity. This is the Senior Psalm, addressing the uncertainties of living in the winter of life.

In the first verse, the senior saint requests that he not be put to shame. In verse 4, he does not want to be squeezed by the hand of the wicked one. In verse 7, he does not want to become a sign to many, a portent, an omen, a black cloud in the sky. And in verse 9, he pleads that he will not end up a castaway, depleted of strength and considered God-forsaken. In these early verses of the psalm, the author clearly communicates the challenges of his senior years.

Who comes to the rescue of the senior citizen as he faces these many challenges? The resounding answer is found throughout the psalm. The LORD is his refuge (v. 1), his rock and fortress (vv. 2-3), his hope since his youth (v.

5), indeed, from the womb (v. 6). This saint boasts of a LORD who is sovereign (v. 16), and who stands as his righteousness (v. 19). Calvin said of this verse,

> *This does not here denote the free gift by which He reconciles men to Himself, or by which He regenerates them to newness of life; but His faithfulness in keeping His promises.*

The solution to the senior's dilemma resides in the person of God, who is a refuge, a rock, a fortress, a hope, the sovereign, the righteous, the restorer, and the Holy One of Israel.

In verse 20, he portrays the Lord as his restorer. In verse 22, the Lord is the Holy One of Israel. There is a solution to the senior's dilemma, and it resides in the person of God who is a refuge, a rock, a fortress, a hope, the sovereign, the righteous, the restorer, and the Holy One of Israel.

What is the lifestyle of the senior citizen? We find the senior saint of the psalm praying (vv. 1-4), trusting (v. 6), and praising the Lord (v. 8). We are reminded of Augustine's words, "A Christian should be an alleluia from head to foot!" He is hoping (v. 14), proclaiming (v. 16), and passing it on (v. 18), leaving his legacy to the next generation. The Senior Psalm conveys that it is possible to be a lifetime apprentice in God's kingdom. The learning never has to conclude and the service to God never has to end!

In this era following the resurrection of Jesus Christ, the contemporary Christian serves a Savior who is present in all seasons. In an age when so many commitments have a short shelf life, every disciple of Jesus Christ can be encouraged that He will be with us to the end of the age (Matthew 28:20). Our Lord is present with every Christian in the winter of his or her life. Truly He is *Immanuel*, God with us, even when the leaves have fallen off the trees and the snow covers the landscape of our lives.

Thought

The answer to the question, "What will be the quality of the winter years of my life?" also answers the question, "Will I walk through those December days with Jesus Christ?"

Prayer

Dear Heavenly Father,

When my senior season comes, I still want to be faithful and bear fruit. I ask humbly that Your Holy Spirit would be strong in me and that Jesus would lead me through the latter days of my earthly journey. Let my despair dissolve in the reality of Your presence and promises.

DAY 21 ~ PSALM 73

My Highest Desire

Whom have I in heaven but you?
And earth has nothing I desire besides you.
(Psalm 73:25)

Asaph led one of King David's Levitical choirs. He is the author of Psalm 73 and within its boundaries he wrestles with one of the most troublesome and debilitating questions the believer faces: "Why do the wicked have it so good?"

The wicked men of his day had the "wish list" of the righteous. They were prosperous, their bodies were healthy, they appeared free from the common burdens of man, people turned to them for advice and counsel, and they personified success.

These positive realities for the ungodly of his time disoriented Asaph because, although many of his days were spent seeking to pursue God and to follow His commandments, he could not claim as much prosperity and apparent favor as those who disobeyed the Lord!

How do the children of God cope with the contemporary blessings of non-believers who flaunt their success before them? It is no easy task, as evidenced by Asaph's honest and transparent confession. In verse 13, he goes as far as to say that it is not worth anything to invest in a pure heart or to keep one's hands clean!

However, by the end of his writings he has changed his opinion and reaffirmed that the Lord is the most valuable asset of his life, and the pursuit of God's will is the greatest and most worthy adventure of his life. What changed him?

81

The attitude of the heart determines the character of the life. Asaph's heart moves back and forth throughout the psalm. He declares that the Lord is good to the pure in heart (v. 1), but he will declare heart purity as vanity (v. 13). Asaph describes his heart as grieved and embittered (v. 21), but he later proclaims that God is the strength of His heart (v. 26). Which is it, Asaph?

The circumstances of life will endeavor to seduce us away from God, but the believer whose heart is set upon the Lord will not wither in the adversities of life, but will rise above them and move beyond them.

If we reflect on our own personal experience, it is both! The heart is moved by the circumstances of life, sometimes to despair, sometimes to delight. At times the believer wavers, at other times the believer is as strong as steel in his commitment to God. The circumstances of life will endeavor to seduce the believer away from God, but the believer who turns to God, whose heart is set upon the Lord, who makes his way to the sanctuary (v. 17), who comes to an understanding of God's nature—that believer will not wither during the adversities of life, but will rise above them and move beyond them.

Asaph, though disturbed by pagan prosperity, would shift his focus from the horizontal to the vertical, from the things which men possessed, to the benefits of his God. When he focused on God, he knew that the Lord was always with him (v. 23). The Lord was his guide in this life (v. 24), and even into the glory of the life to come (v. 24).

The choir director declared that the Lord was the strength of his life (v. 26), and the ever-present refuge of his existence (v. 28). Asaph teaches us to look beyond the obvious to the actual!

The saints of every generation struggle with the luxury and leisure of the non-believer. But Asaph reminds us that we must have the long view of profit and loss. He shows us the ultimate destruction of these who were independent and resistant to God's love. He describes them as on slippery ground (v. 18), and as phantoms and fantasies (v. 20).

It is so imperative to remember that we are grasped by God's right hand (v. 23), guided by His counsel (v. 24), and chauffeured by Him into His glory (v. 24)! At the intersections of our lives we must hold Him highest, value Him as the best, and trust Him most! In the end, the believer wins! Don't settle for second best.

Thought

The answer to the question, "Who or what is *first* in my life?" also answers the question, "Who or what is *second* in my life?"

Prayer

Dear Sovereign Lord,

Keep me from judging a man's prosperity by what he holds in his hand or what he has in his bank account. You can do whatever You want, whenever You want to, with whomever You desire. I ask that You would sustain me when times are lean and remind me that You are the source of all that I have when times are good.

DAY 22 ~ PSALM 84

An Appetite for God

> How lovely is your dwelling place,
> O LORD Almighty!
> My soul yearns, even faints,
> for the courts of the LORD;
> my heart and my flesh cry out
> for the living God. (Psalm 84:1-2)

*A*ll of us have longed for something or someone in our lives. This longing was translated into a heated desire, and we found ourselves interrupting others to talk about the object of our desire. This longing crystallized our strategy. This longing, in plain and simple terms, took over our lives.

In August of 2000, over a hundred trapped sailors had a desperate longing for something—oxygen. A Russian nuclear submarine, the *Kursk*, was disabled below the surface in the Barents Sea. Fresh air was normally supplied by power from the ship's nuclear reactor, but when the reactor stopped functioning, the air stopped flowing. Five hundred feet below the surface, one hundred men were not just wishing, not just hoping, but longing with the drive of a drug addict, to satisfy their need for air.

In this psalm, the sons of Korah have provided for us the story of a man who is trapped in a circumstance that prohibits him from satisfying the desperate drive of his heart, namely, to dwell in the presence of God. For whatever reason—and we cannot be certain of the reason—he is not permitted or is unable to make the journey to the temple to worship God. This man longs, yearns, even is about to faint, because he cannot satisfy the hunger and thirst of his soul. He has an appetite not only for God, but also for the place where God is worshipped. This is the addiction of his life, to gather and glorify God with his brothers and sisters of the faith.

Fortunately, there is free access to God, and in our country, free access to the place where saints gather to worship. Access is not the problem, but the attitude of the heart may be. Let's journey through this psalm to harvest the incredible spirit of the writer, and recommit to have this spirit resident in our own hearts, minds and daily agendas.

If God is Almighty, and He is, this Almighty One can change our bankruptcy into bounty, our catastrophe into a cause for celebration, and death into life.

The description of the Lord as Almighty brings contrast to the forefront, for the writer is in a state of dire need. But if God is Almighty, and He is, this Almighty One can change our bankruptcy into bounty, our catastrophe into a cause for celebration, and death into life, which is quite the metamorphosis.

If you have been in love, you have experienced the insatiable thirst for relationship with your lover. If you have ever run out of water on a humid July day, you have experienced a yearning for ice water. If you have ever been in the hospital for more than a week, you have known firsthand the desire to be home. Our psalmist has known that type of hunger and thirst, and has an appetite, not only for the person of God, but for the place where God is revered and worshipped.

The psalmist is reminded of the small and tiny sparrows that rest in the eaves of the temple (v. 3). This memory sparks even more praise of the place where the Lord is worshipped. At the moment he cannot be there, but he pronounces a blessing upon all those who are dwelling there, and ever praising God.

The word for "those" in verse 5 is *adam* (man). Two commendations are given: (1) the searcher's strength is found in his God; (2) the searcher's heart is set on the pilgrimage.

Baca in verse 6 is similar to the verb "to weep." The singular of the word is translated "balsam trees" or "aspens," which are trees that grow in dry, arid places. They dig blessings out of hardship, which is like digging a well in the desert, so that others can be refreshed.

God continues to supply the psalmist's needs, and so his strength continues to be replenished by God. The pilgrim resorts to prayers and returns to the theology of an omnipotent, all-powerful, Almighty God.

This longing disciple inserts another incredible statement: "Better is one day in your courts than a thousand elsewhere" (v. 10). He would rather spend one day in the temple than two years and nine months outside the temple.

In verse 11 the focus is switched from the king who is a shield, to the Lord who is a sun and shield. The word, Almighty, resurfaces in verse 12, "O LORD Almighty, blessed is the *adam* [man] who trusts in you."

How can the modern-day saint satisfy this longing in his soul? Here is a five-step application for those who hunger and thirst after God and the place where His people gather to worship Him: (1) Cultivate a lifestyle of worship; (2) Prepare for worship; (3) Talk to others about worship; (4) Pray for God's visitation in worship; (5) Be at worship.

Thought

The answer to the question, "How hungry and thirsty am I for the presence of God?" also answers the question, "How full of God will my life be?"

Prayer

O Lord Almighty,

I cannot live without You. You are the supreme object of my heart, the primary Person of my life! I rejoice that You have accepted me and drawn me close to Yourself through the Lord Jesus Christ. Lead me often to Your house and sprinkle me, indeed, shower me with Your glory!

DAY 23 ~ PSALM 90

Life Span

Teach us to number our days aright,
that we may gain a heart of wisdom.
(Psalm 90:12)

At Asbury Seminary the Dean of Students made a statement that has stuck like glue to the fabric of my mind. Dr. Robert Traina, speaking to what makes a man successful, answered with a two-fold response: "Time and how you use it!"

Time is an exasperating aspect of life. You can't delay the clock or speed it up. You can't buy time or give it away. You can't alter the hours in a day; everyone has twenty-four. It is as if a delivery person arrives daily at the front door of our life and deposits a package containing twenty-four hours. No one's day is longer than another's. No one's day is shorter than another's. Time is a very inelastic commodity. And yet it is a commodity. It is invested and spent for different purposes and to attain different goals.

Time is the topic of Psalm 90. Written by Moses, it is the oldest of the psalms, and contrasts the eternity of God with the limited tenure of man. It reveals three aspects of God in relation to time, then proceeds to depress us with a steady diet of unflattering analogies about how much time we really have on this planet. It closes with a needed prayer that we might number our days and spend them for God.

It is said that time passes, but actually, we pass and time stays. I've said, "Time flies," but according to this psalm, man flies and time is merely the instrument by which he measures his flight. In the life span that God allows, how will you invest this unpurchasable commodity?

One of the most impressive characteristics of God is His eternal nature. Food spoils, warranties run out, deciduous trees lose their leaves, and even evergreens eventually turn to "ever-browns." Books fade in color, carpets lose their pile, and records lose their crisp sound. Men and women pass their prime and go through constant metamorphosis; "getting older" does not always mean getting better. In contrast, God is not born, nor will He ever age.

The first two verses of Psalm 90 describe Him as in time, before time, and after time. Moses points out to us that God is the dwelling place of His people in every generation. No portion of the human caravan found God not at home. No searcher ever discovered a "no vacancy" sign. God has always been in attendance and the Divine continuum is a salient fact of human history.

The author informs us that God was before time when he states, "Before the mountains were born or you brought forth the earth and the world" (v. 2). Race back to a time when the great forests sprung up from nature's womb and you will find God. He is the First Cause of all creation.

In glorious contrast is the imagery that God is from everlasting to everlasting. He not only escorts time into being, He bids it farewell. It is God who will tuck time into the scrapbook of history and then nurture His people when they need not wear a watch anymore.

Moses makes a phenomenal statement concerning how God counts time in verse 4. A thousand years is but a 24-hour period in the eyes of God. On this scale, a 100-year life is equivalent to living 144 minutes. Time is not God's master, but His servant. And we sing so emphatically, "When the trumpet of the Lord shall sound and time shall be no more." Time is mortal in contrast to an eternal, everlasting, endless Deity!

The contrast between God's eternity and man's finality is a harsh one to say the least. Verses 3 through 11 casts man into the most lowly and pathetic of analogies. Man is destined to destruction. The translation of the Hebrew in verse 3 could be rendered, "Man is turned to dust." He is sent back to elements, to the habitat of worms. He is ground into the powder of the ground, just as at a burial the minister will say, "Ashes to ashes, dust to dust."

Man is not compared to an oak tree or a blue spruce, but rather to grass. Grass is pretty common fare. It boasts of life in the early morning dew but drags its posture in the afternoon sun. It is easily mowed down, and so life's scythe cuts through man's existence like a hot knife through soft butter.

A third analogy is found in verse 9, where man's life is compared to a tale that is told. The story is so quickly over; the book is so soon closed. It is only yesterday that we remember our teen years; it was only last night that we were married. It was only this morning that we cradled our children . . . and now the nest has emptied.

To make it worse, Moses puts a specific tenure on human life. He lived 120 years, so this is not to say that 70 or even 80 is a maximum, but when you think of your life and if you have reached these plateaus, you realize you have far more behind you than ahead of you. Life is a weaver's shuttle, a vapor that passes away. Shakespeare put it this way:

> *Life's but a walking shadow, a poor player*
> *That struts and frets his hour upon the stage,*
> *And then is heard no more; it is a tale*
> *Told by an idiot, full of sound and fury,*
> *Signifying nothing.*[1]

The Apostle Paul put it this way: "If only for this life we have hope in Christ, we are to be pitied more than all men" (1 Corinthians 15:19).

Our lives also are subject to sinful passions which lead to sinful deeds which lead to the strong and stormy wind of the wrath of God. So the brevity of our lives is compounded by the burden of our sins and the resulting discipline. Verses 7, 9, and 11 will not let us forget the anger and wrath and indignation of this eternal God!

There is a gleam of hope, a ray of light in Moses' prayer which comprises the last eight verses. It gets better. You can spend days of heaven on earth. The finale of Psalm 90 is a gift-wrapped petition to God to assist us in the spending of our days and the investment of the commodity of time in such a manner that God is glorified and we are secure in Him.

"Teach us to number our days." That phrase is not telling us to count how many days we have left, but to carefully evaluate how we live and use the time God does give to each of us! He expects dividends. We will enjoy life if we are accumulating dividends—not the gains of silver and gold, but of incorruptible things.

Only one life, 'twill soon be past,
Only what's done for Christ will last.

Thought

The answer to the question, "Did you invest the days of your life wisely?" also answers the question, "Did you ask the Lord to teach you how to use your days?"

Prayer

Dear Lord of time and eternity,

The sands of time are sinking in the hourglass of my life but your existence is everlasting. You have lived through every generation and You have witnessed every circumstance and situation. Be my mentor in time management so that my days may reap dividends for You and for the Lord Jesus, Your Son and my Savior and Coming King!

Notes

1. William Shakespeare, *Macbeth* V, v, 17.

Day 24 ~ Psalm 91

Under His Wings

He will cover you with his feathers,
and under his wings you will find refuge;
his faithfulness will be your shield and rampart.
(Psalm 91:4)

G. Campbell Morgan called Psalm 91 "one of the greatest possessions of the saints." Charles Spurgeon proclaimed, "There is not a more cheering psalm." This is a psalm where there are no depths or depressions. It is a continuous celebration of God's providence and protection. It begins in verse 1 with a riveting thought: "He who dwells in the shelter of the Most High will rest in the shadow of the Almighty." This word "dwells" can be translated "lodges" or "makes oneself at home." Men and women who spend significant chunks of time in the presence of the Holy One are protected and provided for by their landlord, namely, the Lord God Almighty.

The word "shadow" in verse 1 denotes nearness and proximity, a reminder that God is never remote. Our God is a refuge, a fortress, a bodyguard who can keep me no matter who attacks me. If God wants to keep me safe, no one or nothing can get near me; if God allows me to be vulnerable, I can keep no one or nothing away. This God provides 24-hour security. This is a God who stands sentinel in the day season and in the night season. His alarm systems and security personnel work around the clock and are so devoted to me that they will never leave.

Our God is resilient and tenacious in the care of His children. As we read this psalm of protection, insulation and security, we find that we are under the wings of God (v. 4), which are helping, healing and hiding wings. In verse 7, we find God can insulate those that He chooses in the midst of a frenzied battle. In verse 9, we find that if we make Him our refuge, then we have the promise of verse 10, "then no harm will befall you, no disaster will come near your tent."

We should not deliberately put ourselves in jeopardy just to see God take us out of the fiery furnace. But we do have heavenly bodyguards: "The angel of the LORD encamps around those who fear him, and he delivers them."

This does not suggest that we can deliberately put ourselves in jeopardy. Notice when Satan tempted our Savior in the wilderness, he deployed verses 11-12 to solicit Jesus' participation in putting Himself in harm's way so that God could deliver Him. This is a misuse of this wonderful provision of protection. Indeed, Jesus had the imperial guard of heaven nearby. But, we are not to deliberately put ourselves in jeopardy and to flirt with fire just to see God take us out of the fiery furnace. But we do have heavenly bodyguards as we are reminded in Psalm 34:7: "the angel of the LORD encamps around those who fear him, and he delivers them."

Two conditions are woven into the tapestry of this lovely hymn near its completion. The first is in verse 14: "'Because he loves me,' says the LORD, 'I will rescue him.'" And in verse 15, we find the second: "He will call upon me, and I will answer him." Prayer is a privilege and also it contains tremendous power because when we call upon God, we are given access to His resources and to the ability that He demonstrates to deliver his children. In verse 16, the final, climactic verse, we discover this incredible promise: "With long life will I satisfy him and show him my salvation."

An article in National Geographic several years ago provided a penetrating picture, especially in regard to the pictorial phrase under his wings:

After a forest fire in Yellowstone National Park, forest rangers began their trek up a mountain to assess the inferno's damage. One ranger found a bird literally petrified in ashes, perched statuesquely on the ground at the base of the tree.

Somewhat sickened by the eerie sight, he knocked over the bird with a stick. When he struck it, three tiny chicks scurried from under their dead mother's wings.

The loving mother, keenly aware of impending disaster, had carried her offspring to the base of the tree and had gathered them under her wings, instinctively knowing that the toxic smoke would rise. She could have flown to safety but had refused to abandon her babies.

When the blaze had arrived and the heat had scorched her small body, the mother had remained steadfast. Because she had been willing to die, those under the cover of her wings would live.

"He will cover you with his feathers, and under His wings you will find refuge" (Psalm 91:4). As His children we are the benefactors of His protecting and nurturing love; that should make a huge difference in how we respond and react to the challenges of our lives. Remember the One who loves you, and then be different because of it.

Thought

The answer to the question, "Where are you hiding?" also answers the question, "How secure are you?"

Prayer

Dear Lord,

You are my refuge and fortress, my safe haven and hiding place. Keep me safe in the sunshine and in the storms of my life. Protect, provide and purify my life. Thank you for being accessible to my cries and calls of distress and need.

DAY 25 ~ PSALM 96

When Exclusive Is Not Sheik

Sing to the LORD a new song;
sing to the LORD, all the earth.
(Psalm 96:1)

T his psalm could be labeled, "The Great Missionary Hymn of the Bible." The call sounds far and wide for a *global praise gathering*, embracing every continent, every nation, every people, every language—indeed, every person. The first verse of the psalm immediately shuttles the reader to this worldwide rendition of praise. The concept of "new song" points to recent victories and fresh deliverances that demand more and unique praises.

This serves as a remedial lesson for all believers, for often the praise that used to burst from our lips so naturally and frequently in years past, slows from a flood to a trickle. What new song can you sing today because of divine moments that have brought you new opportunities and recent answers to your prayers? According to verse 2 of the psalm, this "planetary praise" is to be perpetual.

The sweeping song of praise continues to be featured in verse 3, which gives the imperative to "declare His glory among the nations." The psalm constitutes a Missions Manifesto and bids every congregation and every believer to reconsider the Great Commission (Matthew 28:19-20) and the brightness of the missionary flame which should burn in our hearts. This is no time for missionary recruits to dwindle and missionary offerings to shrink. The heart of

God and by extension, the heart of His people, must be intentional toward winning the world!

The psalm takes a different turn beginning in verse 4, when the psalmist deals with the question, "Why should we sing to this Deity?" The answer comes in various forms. He is great and is to be feared above all other gods. In other words, He stands alone; He is in a different league. The diminutive is employed by the psalmist in verse 5 when he states, "For all the gods are idols," which could be translated, "for all the nothings are idols." These idols have been made, but the LORD has made the heavens—quite a contrast.

> *Each generation must decide to worship the One True God, or to worship "idols for destruction."*

Each generation must deal with the issue of who or what will be worshipped, revered, adored. Each generation must decide to worship the One True God, or to worship what Herbert Schlossberg designated as "idols for destruction." If we trace the investment of our time, talents, and treasure, will it lead us to God or gods?

What should we ascribe to the Lord? What should be identified with Him? All the nations—no exceptions—are to ascribe to Him glory and strength, because *glory is due Him!* The recipients of this psalm are to comply with five responses:

Bring an offering
Come into his courts
Worship the Lord in His holiness
Tremble
Say, "The Lord Reigns"

In verses 11 and 12 the invitation is extended to the heavens to rejoice, the earth to be glad, the sea to resound. Above humanity, below humanity, and with humanity, there is to be the glad and ubiquitous song of praise and thanksgiving. Fields are to be jubilant and the trees of the forest are to sing. This is a diverse and sundry symphony and chorus that directs its worship and gratitude to the great God.

The final verse of the psalm flashes the yellow caution light: "for he comes . . . to judge the earth." Make no mistake, God will meet His entire schedule and there will be a trial, with its pardons and its punishments. It is a time to sing; it is also a time to send others or to go ourselves to the nations, so that the choir is complete, all sections are full. Wesley remarked, "The world is my parish." The global glory song will only take place when the hearts of God's children beat with His love and passion for lost people! How can they sing to God if they have never heard of Him? Let the choir recruitment ministry take on a new zeal and purpose!

Thought

The answer to the question, "Do I care if the whole world sings to the Lord?" also answers the question, "Do I understand the heart of God?"

Prayer

Dear Great and Glorious Lord,

I want to declare Your glory across the street and across the sea. Please give me opportunity to share in the winning and building of men and women in my local fellowship and in global missionary endeavors. May my living and my giving be an accurate reflection of Your love and passion for lost people near and far.

Don't Forget the Benefits

Praise the LORD, O my soul,
and forget not all His benefits.
(Psalm 103:2)

G. Campbell Morgan labeled this piece of literature "the perfect psalm of praise." It is a psalm that spells out some of the incredible benefits that the Lord provides for those who love Him and who access His magnanimous grace. For those who embrace its diverse and sundry reminders of how much God lavishes upon a fallen race, it becomes a motivational message to draw the believer nearer and tighter to Him in dynamic relationship.

The psalm debuts in verse 1 with the word "praise," which means, in the original Hebrew, "to kneel, to bless, to salute." The reader is invited to reach deep into the chambers of his soul and exalt the Provider of so many undeserved favors. The second verse gives instruction that the recipient of the blessings should not be forgetful of what this benevolent and loving God has done.

Verse 3 begins to detail this lavish litany of benefits that reach and enhance the life of the worshipper who was once a rebel. The double use of the word "all" emphasizes the absoluteness of the benefits in reference to the (1) forgiveness of our sins and (2) the healing of the diseases that attack our mortal frames. There are no indelible stains on our soul; there are no unhealable diseases in the human portfolio.

Verse 4 presents a quick and stark contrast. The imagery of slavery and royalty race the reader from the depths of the pit to the pinnacle of the throne room of royalty. We are redeemed from our self-imposed bondage and we are crowned with love and compassion.

The benefit package of the Lord touches the physical realm again in verse 5. As our desires are satisfied that leads to our youth being renewed like the eagle's.

---

*The Lord is attracted to the "down
and outers," while many in this world
are attracted to the "up and inners."
Divinity does not divorce itself from
the oppressed; divinity attaches itself
to the oppressed—Hallelujah!*

The welcome recital of blessing continues in verse 6 with the featured thought that the Lord is attracted to the "down and outers," whereas so many in this world are attracted to the "up and inners." This divine proclivity is flagrant in the life of Jesus as He hears the caustic criticism shelled out by the Pharisees that He befriends tax collectors and sinners. Divinity does not divorce itself from the oppressed; divinity attaches itself to the oppressed—Hallelujah!

Verse 7 discloses the crucial fact that the God we worship desires to reveal Himself not only to great leaders like Moses, but also to the masses, the common crowd that makes up His family. He does this through natural theology, the prophets, the Law, circumstances, the voice and impulse of the Holy Spirit, and through the visible picture of the Invisible God, Jesus Christ. The Creator intensely intends for His creatures to know Him!

Verses 8-12 paint a portrait of His incomparable, steadfast love. These verses compose a mini-seminar on the love of God. His anger does not come to a boil quickly, but slowly, for it is mixed with compassion and grace. His love does not manifest itself with persistent anger, but with short-lived disappointment. He does not deal out justice as we truly deserve it; He shortchanges the wages we deserve for our iniquities, the perversities of our lifestyle. How great is His love! Extreme analogies are deployed. As high as the heavens are above the earth describes the love He endows on those who fear Him. As far as the east is from the west measures how far He removes our transgressions from the souls that were stained by them—Hallelujah!

Is it any surprise that those who pursue an understanding of the personality and provisions of God so often end up singing and worshipping and extolling Him! Go ahead —bless the Lord! Pause right now and start applauding His benefits.

Thought

The answer to the question, "Why should I invest my time in praising God?" also answers the question, "What are His many benefits?"

Prayer

My Compassionate and Gracious Lord,

I want to dig deep in the inner part of my soul and excavate great praise and glory to You for the many benefits You escort to my life. Your love is immeasurable and Your anger is slow to burn toward me. Please accept my gratitude, though it is meager payment for the blessings of my life!

DAY 27 ~ PSALM 118

Thanksgiving Has Hindsight and Foresight

Give thanks to the LORD, for he is good;
his love endures forever.
(Psalm 118:1)

Psalm 118 chooses to look back and look forward, to take heart from the past and to look with a strong heart to the future. Martin Luther, the catalyst for the Protestant reformation, labeled this passage as "my chosen psalm," and described it as "the psalm nearest to my heart."[1] It is a thanksgiving hymn, which begins and ends with the theme of thanks. It is a Messianic hymn, because it foreshadows the advent and ministry of Jesus Christ. And it is a liturgical hymn, which has been employed at the time of Passover and is perfectly suited for one group answering another; it is a textbook psalm for a cantor to lead and direct a congregation.

The first four verses serve as a call to worship. There is public praise: "Let Israel say" (v. 2); there is priestly praise: "let the house of Aaron say" (v. 3); and there is personal praise: "let those who fear the Lord say" (v.4). And the content of the praise is, "his love endures forever." The Hebrew word for love, *hesed*, points to a steadfast, resilient love, one that has no built-in obsolescence.

The writer of the psalm quickly conveys that his journey with Jehovah has been no ride in the park. Verse 5 details his anguished cry to the Lord. You could technically translate the phrase "in my anguish" as "out of the narrow

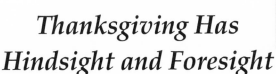

gorge." A colloquial way to translate it would be "between a rock and a hard place." Nevertheless, the author races from anguish to admiration, and his conclusion is liberating: "he answered by setting me free."

This believer makes a pertinent set of choices in verses 8 and 9: "It is better to take refuge in the Lord" than to trust in man or princes. And despite being surrounded and ringed by his enemies (vv. 10-12), and despite being pushed to his limits, "about to fall" (v. 13), he found man's extremity to be God's opportunity!

His thanksgiving then looks back to the deliverance God gave to Israel in Egypt. Verse 14 is an exact quote from Exodus 15:2, which is the victory song of the Israelites after the Lord drowned the Egyptians at the Red Sea. But he not only remembers the troubles and triumphs of the past, he looks to the future, a future which promises to display the same deliverance that God is glorified for in the writer's scrapbook.

The two words, "save us," in verse 25, are a translation of the word, *hosanna*. And the psalmist looks to the Lord to act redemptively in his future and "give him success." This traveler expects more victories and more scrapbook memories to be forthcoming. His dreams are bigger than his memories. Are your dreams bigger than your memories? Is the best yet to come?

This "Hosanna" looks forward to Palm Sunday, to Jesus' entry into the city of Jerusalem, as He prepares to conquer sin and even the final enemy—death! Yes, one day the stone which the builders threw away would become the cornerstone, the cohesive stone, the foundational stone. Look back over your life and reflect upon the "rock and hard place" times and remember how the Lord brought you through the narrowest of alleys. And then, dream and envision a future where He comes again to bring strength, songs, and salvation. Look back, look forward!

Thought

The answer to the question, "Are my dreams bigger than my memories?" also answers the question, "Who is my refuge and the supreme object of my trust and hope?"

Prayer

Dear Lord,

You are the God of my past, present, and future. You command the consequences and results of all the tenses in my history. Thank you for love that is resilient, that endures forever. Make my life a resonating song of praise that proclaims Your reality and redemption to my family and friends.

Notes

1. From the Dedication of Luther's translation of Psalm 118.

DAY 28 ~ PSALM 119

Preventing the Fumble and the Fall

How can a young man keep his way pure?
By living according to your word.
I seek you with all my heart;
do not let me stray from your commands.
I have hidden your word in my heart
that I might not sin against you.
(Psalm 119:9-11)

The 119th Psalm is not a favorable choice for after-dinner devotions. It is the "Granddaddy Psalm," comprising 22 eight-verse sections, equaling almost two dozen of the normal psalms in length. It has been called the "Hebrew Alphabet Psalm" because the 22 sections correspond to the 22 letters in the Hebrew language and each section starts with a word beginning with the first letter of the alphabet, and then the second letter, and so on in consecutive order, until the whole alphabet has been given representation.

The Word of God is elevated in this psalm to heights that are not equaled in any other portion of Scripture. Eight synonyms are used for the Word of God and they appear in all but one of the 176 verses. If you read and meditate upon this psalm you will sense a new dimension of gratitude for God's revelation to man and its potential to impact and drastically alter the course of your history!

In verses 9-16 the writer grapples with the issue of sin and its defilement, and what role the Word of God can play in preventing sin and its affliction. Long ago I inscribed in my Bible this little axiom: "Sin will keep me from this book, or this book will keep me from sin!" As you learn to understand the faith, you realize that this statement cannot hold water without some leakage, but for the most part, its truth can render significant gains in the spiritual formation of our lives.

This second segment of Psalm 119 discloses the powerful and prevailing possibilities if Scripture becomes incorporated into the life and work of the believer. In an age characterized by a frantic pace and misplaced priorities, modern man has for the most part shelved daily communion with God. In essence, he is too busy and too independent to get "back to the Bible."

The opening verse of this section poses the question of how a young man can "keep his way pure" (v. 9). The Hebrew word for young, *naar*, can be translated "shaken off" and would seem to indicate that time in life when a person becomes more dependent on himself than on his parents. This span of life, from God's vantage point, is precarious. Young men and women can stain their lives, alter their course, and mortgage their future with just a few falls or one major leap. Purity of heart and cleansing of soul can occur by living according to God's Word. The Bible does not have all the answers, but it does have the most important ones.

There is disdain for this book today, and consequently there are lives being blown apart by sin and its empty promises. The Bible is the "Manufacturer's manual." This is the compass which points you in the right direction. This is the navigator's chart that does not reveal where all the sandbars are located, but as the old captain said, "I know where the channel is, and that will get me safely home."

Are we sensitive to temptation, the traps of Satan, and the ambushes of those who would seek to manipulate our lives and squeeze holiness right out of our souls? Verse 11 tells us that a heart saturated with the Word is less likely to stumble and fall short of God's standard.

At today's airports, much attention is directed at detecting metal objects being carried onto planes. As I recently went through this process, I was a witness to the harsh buzzer which indicated that indeed there was something to be watched and weighed as to its appropriateness. The ability of these metal detectors to uncover bombs and weapons has spared many a traveler an appointment with death.

I believe that a revival of attention to God's Word would lead to massive reforms in our daily living patterns; it is God's "metal detector" to make us sensitive to unrighteousness in our lives, which can be more dangerous than any bomb or weapon. God dares you to try it and see.

Psalm 119:13 is a litmus test of our interaction with God's Word. The more we absorb it, the more often we declare it! The world is crowded with people groping in darkness, and as we declare God's Word we diffuse light. Later in this psalm it says, "Your word is a lamp to my feet and a light for my path" (v. 105).

In our affluent culture verse 14 is extremely difficult to put into practice. The worshipper writes that the testimonies of God are equal to the riches that he possesses. In ministering to a church executive's dying wife I was given a rare jewel from her pale lips. She said, "The things I thought were important don't seem as important anymore, and those things I put off now seem to be the most important!" A deep appreciation for God's Word is not something you schedule for retirement or the dismal days of a terminal illness. Grasp the joy of the Word that daily brings festive faith and often convicting challenge to your doorstep.

Will you consider these affirmations in your own life? It doesn't take a voice from heaven or even a miracle to begin to participate in the serious study of God's Word. And it may prevent a catastrophic free fall in your life that causes irreparable damage.

Thought

The answer to the question, "Do I daily use the Word of God as my compass for life?" also answers the question, "How often do I get lost on my journey?"

Prayer

Dear Heavenly Father,

I am so grateful that You have provided a compass for my life. Your Word is a lamp to my feet and a bright light to my path. Create in me a greater appetite for Your Truth so that I may avoid detours and distractions. Prompt me to persist in the hiding of Your Word in my heart!

Running into God

> *Where can I go from your Spirit?*
> *Where can I flee from your presence?*
> *If I go up to the heavens, you are there;*
> *if I make my bed in the depths, you are there.*
> *(Psalm 139:7-8)*

The story is told of a secular philosopher who asked, "Where is God?" One Christian answered, "Let me first ask, where is He not?"

David, the writer of Psalm 139, would have appreciated that response. He had an enormous concept of God. How big is your God? This Scripture passage unlocks a door to an awesome portrait of an Almighty God.

Three adjectives are often used to describe the Judeo-Christian God: *omniscient, omnipresent* and *omnipotent.* Their meanings are not as hard to grasp as they may sound. The prefix "omni" means "all"; the three words mean God is all-knowing, all-present and all-powerful, respectively.

David declares in the early verses of this hymn that he is an "open book" to God; nothing is hidden from Him. David illustrates this inexhaustible bank of God's knowledge with some examples. The Lord knows when David sits down and gets up; all his movements are monitored.

This omniscience extends to, and even anticipates, David's thoughts. Before a thought is even conceived, God knows its color and character. He can read our minds. This can be a blessing, since our motives are often misinterpreted. Our Judge knows what is behind our actions, and may be pleased with us even if others are not. The flip side is that God knows if we are hypocrites. This God knows when my thoughts are royal—and when they are rotten.

David goes on in verse 3, using a literary device known as parallelism (saying the same thing twice). "You discern my going out and my lying down," he says, and adds, "you are familiar with all my ways." These expressions put omniscience on the lowest shelf for us to comprehend.

What about our speech? The answer is the same; God knows every compliment and criticism we utter. He hears every inspirational sentence and every idle word. I got some good advice from an old coal miner in my first pastorate: "Chew your words before you say them." God is listening!

God's omniscience encompasses our lives. He knows where we've been, anticipates where we'll be, and touches our lives in the present. God steps into all three tenses.

David acknowledges in verse 6 that this knowledge is outside human capacity. The air gets really thin when we try to reach this level of understanding; it defies human solution or explanation. A.W. Tozer made a consoling statement on this issue in *The Pursuit of God*:

> *God will not hold us responsible to understand the mysteries of election, predestination, and the divine sovereignty. The best and safest way to deal with these truths is to raise our eyes to God and in deepest reverence say, "O Lord, Thou knowest."*[1]

I must approach life with the confidence expressed in an old hymn: "I don't know about tomorrow, but I know who holds my hand." Both my short-circuited cognition and God's omniscience are givens in this Christian journey!

The all-knowing God is also the omnipresent God! As human beings, we can be in only one place at any time. It is vitally important that we realize God is not spatially limited. He permeates all realms, all space, all existence!

David asks, if he ascends to heaven, to the land of angels, will he separate himself from his Maker? The answer is obvious—no! If he races to the other end of existence, to the land of the dead, does this puts him out of God's reach? The answer again is categorically no! David rides this theological wave even further. What if he rode on the morning clouds, sailed uncharted waters, or dove to the deepest part of the sea? Would God still accompany him and guide him? Yes, his Lord will never leave him nor forsake him!

Omnipresence is taught throughout God's Word, and we must live in the light of this truth. If we sin, there is no use hiding in the bushes, like Adam and Eve. If God gives us a task and we skip town like Jonah, we will find that when we try to run away from God, we run into Him.

This doctrine is made all the sweeter when we see in verses 11-12 that even darkness is like light to God. This is a great comfort to those of us caught in a shroud of spiritual darkness. Whatever your "night season" of life, whether the dark world of a hospital bed, the midnight of a fractured relationship, or the dirty, sunless hovel of some stupid or careless sin, there is hope, for God is near.

David broadens his portrait of God by going back to the days before his birth. The Creator's touch is evident in the dark recesses of a mother's womb. Here, God's eye was on the fetus of David; He supervised the shaping of the embryo and knitted together his unborn body. God reigns even in prehistory! The days of David's life were written in God's book before they were lived. The diary of David was already on God's shelf before his life had even begun.

This view of God's life-giving power is crucial in our age. We have swallowed abortion and choked on God's Word, which clearly speaks of God's activity in the lives of Jeremiah, John the Baptist and David *before* their birth. An all-powerful God is looking out for us! He brought us into this world, sustains us during our pilgrimage, and will rescue us when death's cold wave pulls us under! We are fearfully and wonderfully made, because He is omnipotent!

We are frail children of dust, yet God—the immortal, invisible, only wise God—thinks about us. This is food for praise! Psalm 139:17-18 tells us that God's thoughts of us are more numerous than the grains of sand on the seashore.

David returns to the searching nature of God in verse 23 with the petition, "Search me, O God, and know my heart." My knowledge is fragmented; I need God to search my soul. I sin in many places, but His pervasive presence makes Him accessible to my prayers wherever I utter them. I need power to lead me out of the miry clay and direct me in the narrow way. God, and God alone, can do that for me!

Use the eyes of faith in your life. Use a wide-angle lens to form your view of God—omniscient, omnipresent and omnipotent. He knows, He is here and He can do it all! If He didn't, wasn't and couldn't, He would not be God. I'm grateful He is!

Thought

The answer to the question, "Can I run away from God?" also answers the question, "Is there anywhere God does not dwell?"

Prayer

O Lord,

I am so thankful that nothing escapes Your eyes, that You are everywhere, and that You can do anything that You desire. No height or depth challenges You; no power or force threatens You. I am honored to be watched and cared for by such an awesome God! There are no words adequate to describe You! I worship You and You alone!

Notes

1. A. W. Tozer, *The Pursuit of God* (Camp Hill, PA: Christian Publications, 1982), p. 104.

DAY 30 ~ PSALM 150

Praise the Lord!

Praise the LORD. . . .
Let everything that has breath praise the LORD.
Praise the LORD. (Psalm 150:1, 6)

It is fitting that Psalm 150 is the final composition of the Hebrew hymnbook. It has the stamp of David upon it. The word praise occurs one dozen times. All types of instruments are brought into the celebration of God and His mighty deeds. It is the icing on the cake as David commends his God and expresses his adoration.

I would remind you that David had much to praise the Lord for, such as ascending to the united throne of Israel and Judah, such as slaying the gigantic gladiator from Gath named Goliath, such as loyal soldiers and compassionate courtiers who took care of his health as he aged and withered. He had won many battles, worn many crowns and wooed many beautiful women.

We must never forget, however, that the singer was turned upon by the king he faithfully served. This man was chased all over the Holy Land. One wife mocked his dancing after battle, two sons conspired to kill him, one of his sons raped his own sister, and of course, his humanity caved in to the beauty of Bathsheba, and the result is one of history's most disappointing soap operas.

Yet through it all, David never lost his praise for God!

This patchwork quilt effect is present in our community of faith. As you study church history, it is replete with highs and lows, saints and crooks, feasts and famines, healing and holocausts. That is why we must pursue the imperative, "Praise the Lord!"

There will never be a week that does not reflect the mixed bag of triumph and tragedy, light and darkness. The command, "Praise the Lord," lifts all of us above the circumstances which will shape our smiles and start our tears.

The Psalms, especially, encourage us to maintain an attitude of praise, affirming God's glory and remembering His great and awesome deeds, and forecasting the marvelous ending that He will bring to history.

Each of the last five Psalms begins and ends with *Hallelujah*. The Lord is trying to drive this point home, *He is worthy of praise*, and when all is said and done, praise will be our everlasting theme.

I've seen many people who left a ballgame early because their team seemed hopelessly behind, only to find the next day that their team won! Many a Republican read with joy in the paper the early-edition headline, "Dewey defeats Truman," only to choke the next day on the final result, which declared Truman's comeback and conquest!

The word *hallel*, which is threaded throughout the Psalms, means "to shine, celebrate, or boast." We are to boast of God! Its root meaning is traced to deep, abiding gratitude that points to a superior deed or person. This person is your heavenly Father.

This God transcends space, stretches further than time, and is the Creator, the ultimate Sustainer and Provider of eternal, immeasurable, and incalculable Life!

When you praise Him in the good times, you acknowledge His goodness. But when you praise Him in the bad times, you testify to your trust in Him. Your belief in God will translate into joy in the dark "dog days" of life. When life gives you a lemon, make lemonade! He is in control! He is God and God alone!

The best illustration I can give to close this series on the Psalms, which has occupied parts of my calendar over the last three years, is the experience of a missionary who was traveling by train to Chicago from the West Coast. She had stopped off at Denver to speak, and during the course of her stay, she visited the capital building and was impressed by a beautiful tapestry of the Oregon Trail. As she drew near it, she decided to turn it over and look at the backside of this masterpiece. She was surprised to find knots, tangles, and many dangling strings. How could something so lovely have all of this unsightly appearance? As she rose to a higher level to gaze down on the tapestry, she again saw the front view and it stirred her once more. She realized that when she looked only at the underside, she could never re-alize the splendid elegance of the craftsman's finished product. The point she made is so crucial to our lives: you can look on the wrong side, and be depressed, or by faith you can take the higher view and look by the eyes of faith on the finished product. Life is full of tangles, knots and loose strings, which don't appear to be part of anything beautiful or worthy of praise, but one day we shall look from a higher vantage point at the other side of the tapestry. Praise the Lord! Life is full of tangles, knots and loose strings, but these are part of the tapestry of the Lord!

Thought

The answer to the question, "Do I ever look on the other side of the tapestry?" also answers the question, "Will I miss the work of God?"

Prayer

Dear Lord,

I praise You for Your character and creation! I praise You for all that I know and for all that I can imagine! You are the best of the best, the most excellent, the magnificent God! May my breath be framed in thanksgiving to You, in every day season and night season. I love You deeply and my heart's desire is to adore You forever and ever. Amen.

119

If you would like additional copies of
Psalms for the Seasons of Life,
you may order them at:

http://store.signaturesoundquartet.com
(Click on "Catalog," then "Arnold Fleagle")

or call 330-677-0624

Comments or additional order inquiries may be

made through the following e-mail address:

honeycombhouse@yahoo.com

Thank you for your interest!